Asian Trade and Investment in Europe

This book provides a deep insight into the flow of foreign direct investment from Asia to Europe. It assesses the topic of trade and investment from the reverse direction, considering Asian countries as the capital investors in the EU countries.

Each chapter analyses either the international trade or the investment of one or more Asian countries in correlation with one or more European states. The book analyses a significant number of countries, which are members in various economic associations, such as the Visegrad Group, the Three Seas Initiative, the European Free Trade Association, or are states from the same geopolitical region – for instance, the Iberian Peninsula, Baltic States, and Nordic countries. It examines Indian outward foreign direct investment trends in the UK before and after Brexit, based on select case studies, to emphasize the impact of Brexit, as well as to encourage trade and investment among Asian and European countries before and during COVID-19 to highlight the influence of the pandemic on the target country's economy.

The authors use a variety of analytical methods in the book, such as numerical presentations, econometric analysis, descriptive statistical analysis, an examination of time-series dynamics, the modelling of functions, and semi-structured interviews with company executives. The regional perspectives bring new and useful insights to the topic, and the case study approach allows for a wider exploration of the research questions as well as their theoretical evolution.

The book provides a "big picture" for economists, researchers, business analysts, and PhD students of economics, international trade, and business.

Prana Krishna Biswas is Former Research Dean at the Institute of Management Technology, Ghaziabad, India, and currently Senior Vice President, India, New York Institute of Finance.

Robert Dygas is Assistant Professor in the Department of East Asian Economic Studies at the SGH Warsaw School of Economics, Warsaw, Poland.

Routledge Studies in the Modern World Economy

Regionalism in Latin America
Agents, Systems and Resilience
Edited by José Briceño-Ruiz and Andrés Rivarola Puntigliano

Economic Growth and Convergence
Global Analysis through Econometric and Hidden Markov Models
Michał Bernardelli, Mariusz Próchniak and Bartosz Witkowski

Neoliberalism in the Emerging Economy of India
The Political Economy of International Trade, Investment and Finance
Edited by Byasdeb Dasgupta, Archita Ghosh and Bishakha Ghosh

Asian Foreign Direct Investment in Europe
Edited by Prana Krishna Biswas and Robert Dygas

Economic Policy and the Covid-19 Crisis
The Macroeconomic Response in the US, Europe and East Asia
Edited by Bernadette Andreosso-O'Callaghan, Woosik Moon and Wook Sohn

Industrial Development
How States Build Capabilities and Deliver Economic Prosperity
Greg Clydesdale

Ageing and Effecting Long-term Care in China
Sabrina Ching Yuen Luk, Hui Zhang and Peter P. Yuen

Asian Trade and Investment in Europe
Edited by Prana Krishna Biswas and Robert Dygas

Critical Perspectives on Economics of Education
Edited by Silvia Mendolia, Martin O'Brien, Alfredo Paloyo and Oleg Yerokhin

For more information about this series, please visit: www.routledge.com/Routledge-Studies-in-the-Modern-World-Economy/book-series/SE0432

Asian Trade and Investment in Europe

Edited by Prana Krishna Biswas and Robert Dygas

Institute of Management Technology
Ghaziabad, Delhi NCR

AACSB ACCREDITED

SGH
Warsaw School of Economics

110 1906 2016
WITH HERITAGE TO PROGRESS

Routledge
Taylor & Francis Group
LONDON AND NEW YORK

First published 2022
by Routledge
4 Park Square, Milton Park, Abingdon, Oxon OX14 4RN

and by Routledge
605 Third Avenue, New York, NY 10158

Routledge is an imprint of the Taylor & Francis Group, an informa business

British Library Cataloguing-in-Publication Data
A catalogue record for this book is available from the British Library

Library of Congress Cataloging-in-Publication Data
A catalog record has been requested for this book

ISBN: 978-1-032-22964-5 (hbk)
ISBN: 978-1-032-22966-9 (pbk)
ISBN: 978-1-003-27493-3 (ebk)

DOI: 10.4324/9781003274933

Typeset in Times New Roman
by Apex CoVantage, LLC

Contents

Illustrations

Figures

Tables

Contributors

Prana Krishna Biswas, Former Dean, Institute of Management Technology (IMT), Ghaziabad, India, currently Senior Vice President, India, New York Institute of Finance

Robert Dygas, Assistant Professor, World Economy Research Institute, SGH Warsaw School of Economics, Warsaw, Poland

Sigurður Guðjónsson, University of Iceland, Iceland

Scott Hegerty, Associate Professor, Advisor, Northeastern Illinois University, the USA

Jón Þorvaldur Heiðarsson, University of Akureyri, Iceland

Kai Jia, Associate Professor, University of Electronic Science and Technology of China, Chengdu, China

Martin Kenney, Professor, University of California

Riina Kerner, Estonian Business School, Estonia

Meelis Kitsing, Rector, Professor of Political Economy and Professor of Economics and Finance, Estonian Business School, Estonia

Helga Kristjánsdóttir, Faculty of Business, University of Akureyri, Iceland

Makiko Narita, Associate Professor, Faculty of Economics, University of Nagasaki, Japan

Guðmundur Kristján Óskarsson, University of Akureyri, Iceland

Smita Shukla, Director, Alkesh Dinesh Mody Institute for Financial and Management Studies, University of Mumbai, India

Artur Tomeczek, Global Economic Interdependence Unit, SGH Warsaw School of Economics, Poland

Abbreviations

3SI	Three Seas Initiative
ARDL	Autoregressive Distributive Lag
ARMA	Autoregressive Moving Average
BSFI	Banking, Financial Services and Insurance
BTIA	Broad Based Trade and Investment Agreement
CAI	Comprehensive Agreement on Investment Between China and EU
CBRN	The Defence Chemical, Biological, Radiological and Nuclear Centre
CIED	Counter Improvised Explosive Device
DOTS	The International Monetary Fund's Direction of Trade Statistics
EFTA	European Free Trade Association
EJTC	Estonian Japan Trading Company
EMENA	Europe, Middle East and North Africa
EPA	Economic Partnership Agreement
ERS	Engineering and Research and Development Services
FDIO	Foreign Direct Investment Outbound
FNSR	Foundation for National Security Research
FTA	Free Trade Agreement
GARCH	Generalized Auto-Regressive Conditional Heteroskedasticity
GATS	General Agreement on Trade in Services
GCV	Global Value Chain
GoI	The Government of India
GPC	Good Practices Conference
IPM	Intellectual Property Monetization
ITBS	IT and Business Services
JETRO	Japan External Trade Organization
JLR	Jaguar Land Rover
MHRA	Medicine and Healthcare Product Regulatory Agency
MNC	Multinational corporation
NDICI	Neighbourhood, Development, and International Cooperation Instrument
NPPA	The National Press and Publication Administration
PBG	Platform business group
RBI	Reserve Bank of India
REER	Real Effective Exchange Rate

SAIC	The State Administration for Industry and Commerce
SMETS	Smart Meter Equipment Technical Specifications
STRI	Services Trade Restrictiveness Index
TME	Tencent Music Entertainment
UNSC	United Nations Security Council
V4	Visegrad Group
WEF	World Economic Forum

Preface

This book is the result of a joint effort of academic professionals/authors from European and Asian universities to review the trends in trade and investment flow from Asia to European regions such as Scandinavia, Baltic States, Spain, and chosen CEE countries and to systemize the knowledge in this subject based on the case studies of EFTA Trade Bloc, Visegrad Group, Spain, Baltic countries and the UK. This monograph has the format of a textbook introducing the area of Asian trade and investments in Europe and consists of case studies of selected Asian countries as well as the process of their selection. Chosen Asian countries like China, India, and Japan are the most preferred interest of the authors due to their strategic importance in world economy. The cases in each chapter by the authors give interesting insight and a variety of concepts and outcomes in the global economy. The development of Asian studies and related didactics are very important premise of this publication. The main research question raised in this book is how did the trade and investment among Asian countries and European regions look like during COVID-19 time? The other questions are related to some of the following: (1) Is it beneficial for the EFTA trade bloc to have Free Trade Agreement with China? (2) Which of the European Nordic economies are the most of interest from an Asian ICT trade and investment perspective? (3) What are the effects of COVID-19 and Brexit on the investments of Indian international companies in the UK? (4) What is the role of Visegrad Group in attracting more of Asian trade and investment to Europe? (5) What are the bilateral trade relations among Baltic States and China, Japan and India? (6) What is the impact of Asian trade and investments on the EU economy?

Presented case studies help to answers these questions.

The title of this book focuses mainly on current challenges in Asian trade and investment with Europe. Despite numerous publications on the EU–Asia economic relations, there may be only few studies dedicated to Asian trade and investments in the EU countries in regional perspective including dedicated case studies. It should be emphasized that this is the case despite the fact that a systematic increase in these investments is noted, especially Chinese ones, since 2001. In particular, there are no comprehensive monographs presenting Asian trade and investments in European regions, which would go beyond discussing one case study. This book consists of nine chapters related to Asian trade and investment in

Europe with a regional perspective. **Chapter 1** provides numerical presentation and econometric analysis of the trading effects on individual EFTA countries that started Free Trade Agreements with China in 2014. Macroeconomic data for both exports and imports are analysed, and it is the first time the macroeconomic data is applied like this. For more efficient management decision, measurement and estimation are important. Results are positive for exports from China to EFTA but not for exports from EFTA to China. It is, therefore, not possible to conclude that Free Trade Agreement between the EFTA countries and China will pay off for the European countries – for the time period analysed. What the future holds must be based on speculations considering future measurements. **Chapter 2** explores concrete cases of Nordic technology platforms which have been the recipient of Asian FDI. It does so by relying on semi-structured interviews with company executives and publicly available secondary data. The chapter reveals a considerable heterogeneity depending on investors' origin, underlying incentives, the nature of technology platform as well as the size of investments. The diverse outcomes insist that the context specificity of Asian FDI is crucial for understanding investment patterns rather the one-size-fits-all approach, assuming purely one-sided motivation. **Chapter 3** concludes that trading and investment patterns are different in the sense of service and investment constraints and direction of flows. Estonia, as a digital country, attracts investments with a business-friendly environment and exports knowledge-intensive services to Japan, while Japan, on the contrary, invests much more into other countries, including Estonia. As a result, the trade and investments bring valuable benefits to both countries, including jobs and movement of firms, while including the capital itself together with the transfer of technological know-how and knowledge of foreign markets. **Chapter 4** analyses the evolution of Japanese foreign direct investment in Spain and which kinds of industries have the advantage of attracting Japanese direct investment. The chapter also compares Spain and Poland regarding FDI flow from Japan. After Spain joined the European Union in the 1980s, a lot of foreign companies including Japan located in Iberian countries, mainly in the manufacturing industry. However, when Central and Eastern European countries joined the EU in the 2000s, they were regarded as being promising investment destinations, and some companies relocated from Southern European countries to Central and Eastern European countries. Turrión (2005) concluded that Spain and Portugal were losers in attracting direct investment vis-a-vis Central and Eastern European countries in the industries with technology and knowledge. The methodology used in the chapter is statistical analysis of foreign direct investment flows and stocks provided by JETRO, UNCTAD, and OECD. **Chapter 5** studies the Indian outward foreign direct investment trends in the UK before and after Brexit based on select case studies. According to data from the Department of International Trade (UK), India has been the second-largest foreign direct investor in the UK during the year 2019–20 and 2020–21 and the United States being the first. The foreign direct investment trends reflect the confidence of Indian companies in the UK. The UK and India also have had a historical relationship and several shared values. This chapter presents case studies to analyse the driving factors for the volume of the

Indian direct investment by the UK. The case studies also offer insights into the interest of Indian companies in making direct investments in certain sectors in the UK. Besides this, the chapter also provides a perspective on future trade and investment relations between the UK and India, considering the COVID-19 crisis and Brexit effect. **Chapter 6** describes trade and investment nature and development between India and Visegrad Group (Poland, Hungary, Czech Republic, and Slovakia) and also a description of Visegrad Group Region's position in Europe together with Three Seas Initiative (3SI). It presents main advantages of this region regarding Asian investments, an overview of main documents signed between India and Visegrad Group countries, and an analysis of the advantages each Visegrad country offers for a possibility of future investment. It also presents the important Indian MNCs operating in Visegrad Region, specifying market entry strategies of Indian companies operating in Visegrad Region and showing the sectoral overview. The chapter also discusses the impact of COVID-19 on the potential Indian investments in Visegrad Region. A chosen case study of Tata Motors is presented regarding Indian investment in Slovakia. **Chapter 7** focuses on Chinese digital platforms which have become global competitors in recent years. With a different domestic political economic environment, Chinese digital platforms illustrated an alternative growth model from Silicon Valley model, which was named as "platform business group (PBG)" which is still valid in the global market. First, the tightening anti-trust regulation pressure in global market would possibly impede the capacity of Chinese digital giants to form business groups in which the components might guide traffic to each other. Second, the competition from global giants, especially Silicon Valley, would possibly restrain the capacity of the core platforms to be leveraged to form the PBG model by Chinese digital giants. In this way, how the PBG model would change according to the global markets becomes the central question of this chapter. A case study of Tencent, one of the largest two Chinese digital giants, is presented to answer the question. Given the regulatory institutions in the EU being the most comprehensive and typical across countries, this chapter was especially focused on the expansion of Tencent in the EU. An assembled database of the overseas operations of Tencent in the EU would describe the globalization patterns of it and analyse the strengths of it and obstacles to its globalization here. The chapter concludes with several findings: First, the PBG model is still the choice of Chinese digital giants as it is natural to exploit the common database of the users. Second, the PBG model is largely reduced as the regulation pressure of the local market. Third, Tencent mainly focuses on game industry in the EU rather than social media and payment industry, both of which are most powerful in China. **Chapter 8** focuses on the Baltic countries of Estonia, Latvia, and Lithuania – small open economies which have substantial trade relations with large Asian exporters. The study presented in this chapter examines the time-series dynamics of the monthly bilateral trade balances of each Baltic country with China, India, and Japan from 1999 to 2020. Each trade balance is first divided into separate "regimes" based on structural break tests; these are shown to have significantly different means, and the starting and ending points vary by country. Estonia, for example, went from having a trade deficit versus Japan to having more balanced trade following 2008. Each trade balance is then modelled as a function of domestic and foreign income, the real effective exchange rate (REER), and a GARCH-based measure of REER volatility. Cointegration analysis shows that while each trade balance has different macroeconomic determinants, interesting patterns emerge – particularly regarding India. Closing **Chapter 9** gives an insight into Foreign Direct Investment Outflow (FDIO) of chosen Asian countries to EU-28 nations before coronavirus SARS-Cov-2 (COVID-19) and Brexit. The period of the analysis is based on the available data (2010–2019). The main goal in this chapter is to analyse investment destinations from Asian countries, their impact on the EU economy, and important government initiatives that influenced the global economy in the analysed period. The novelty of this research is a network model approach and an overview of how the FDIO from Asian economies adds value to the EU's economic growth. Due to the lack of data, it is quite difficult to analyse the impacts of COVID-19 and Brexit on the global economy after 2019. However, based on reliable and available projections concerning FDIs, some insight was provided. In this chapter, the network analysis was used and empirical study of available data and a review of world reports as the research methods were used as well. Network analysis identifies the key players in Asia and Europe. Besides that, some updates to the current situation in 2021 are provided based upon observations and the facts regarding changes in FDIO from Asia to the EU with a special focus on the EU economic growth. The chapter concludes that due to COVID-19, FDI flow globally will be reduced by 35–40% in 2020–2021. The EU needs to establish a strategic investment partnership with India as a counterpart to China. China still has a strong economic position in the EU and implements its 2019 policy of Belt and Road Initiative to keep its hegemony by getting over European companies and winning government contracts, and the network analysis reveals four spheres of influence in Europe (Japan/India, Hong Kong/Singapore, China/South Korea, and Thailand).

This book gives the insight on the most crucial challenges of Asian trade and investment with European regions during COVID-19 time, and a distinguishing feature of the book is the accurate selection of the most important case studies.

Prana Krishna Biswas and Robert Dygas

Author biographies

Prof. Prana Krishna Biswas has more than 38 years of experience in Management Education. He started his academic journey with Administrative Staff College of India, Hyderabad in 1983. He has been a Professor at Indian Institute of Forest Management, Bhopal (Govt. of India), Director of Lal Bahadur Shastri Institute of Management, Delhi, and Director of Institute for Financial Management & Research (IFMR), Chennai. In April 2018, he joined as the founding Vice Chancellor of Skyline University, Nigeria – the first private university in North-West Nigeria. From February 2019 to September 2021, he has been Dean (Academics/Research/Special Projects) of IMT, Ghaziabad (Delhi-NCR), which is AACSB accredited institution and a top-ranked premier B-School in India. Currently, w.e.f November 2021, he is Senior Vice President, India, New York Institute of Finance.

He has specialized in Public Policy, Micro Finance, Social Entrepreneurship, Corporate Social Responsibility, Livelihood, Development Management & Sustainability.

He has published more than 50 papers in peer-reviewed journals and three books, and has completed about 55 funded research projects. He is member of several national and international professional institutions and has rich experience in conducting research, management development programs and consulting for World Bank, ADB, SIDA, JICA, Ford Foundation, State Govts, Govt of India and others.

Robert Dygas, Ph.D., is an Assistant Professor in SGH Warsaw School of Economics at East Asian Economic Studies Department of the World Economy Research Institute. He completed his master studies at the Warsaw School of Economics, majoring in Finance and Banking, and at the University of Aarhus in Denmark, majoring in Management. He received his Ph.D. in Economics from the Warsaw School of Economics in 2003 (dissertation: "Strategic Management in the Mobile Telephony Industry in Poland in 1995–2001"). In 2011, he was awarded the Executive Master of Business Administration degree by the Warsaw University of Technology, Business School. He has 23 years of professional experience in multinational corporations in IT, telecommunications, and public sector. In 2015–2020, he worked also as the external expert for evaluation of Horizon 2020-ECI-FTI proposals (Research Executive Agency EASME under the power delegated by the European Commission).

Academic interests: Geoeconomics, Economies of Asian countries.

1 International trade between the EFTA trade bloc and China

Helga Kristjánsdóttir, Guðmundur Kristján Óskarsson, Jón Þorvaldur Heiðarsson, and Sigurður Guðjónsson

Introduction

Within Europe, there are several trading agreements, which are between the EU, EFTA, and the EES. The EU is the European Union and related to EFTA is the European Free Trade Association through the EEA – the European Economic Area (Europe, 2021). Some of the EFTA countries have individual free trade agreements (FTAs) with China. The research question here is "Is it more beneficial for the EFTA countries as a bloc to have some type of trading agreement with China?"

To answer the question, we analysed trading effects on the two EFTA countries of Iceland and Switzerland, having FTAs with China since 2014 (European Free Trade Association, 2021; Óskarsson & Kristjánsdóttir, 2021). Data runs from 2010 through 2016, analysing both exports and imports. The question is highly interesting, China has comparative advantage in the production of various goods. Also, we need to consider the potential link between FDI and economic performance (Hjálmarsdóttir & Kristjánsdóttir, 2022).

The research is based on the gravity model, frequently used in research of trade between countries (Tinbergen, 1962; Pöyhönen, 1963; Bergstrand, 1989), and it appears to work well (Bergstrand, 1989). The model has gained stronger theoretical explanation over the years. Empirical results using the gravity model show more trade between countries if they decrease trade barriers (Bagwell & Staiger, 2005; Subramanian & Wei, 2007; Eicher & Henn, 2011; Kristjánsdóttir, 2013, 2017, 2019a, 2019b, 2021; Kristjánsdóttir et al., 2017, 2020, 2022).

The China trade was stimulated when China joined the WTO in 2001 (Subramanian & Wei, 2007; WTO, 2015). There appears to be more focus on non-EU countries, such as EFTA countries that have alliances with the EU (Lanteigne, 2010). It is therefore a reason to examine whether individual countries in EFTA are better off having FTAs with China or not.

DOI: 10.4324/9781003274933-1

Model setup

Anderson (1979) and Bergstrand (1985) provided theoretical explanation for the gravity model, and the first specification presented here is in log-linear format, as follows:

$$ln\left(Imports\ to\ EFTA_{ij,t}\right) = \omega_0 + \omega_1\, ln\left(GDP_{j,t}\right) + \omega_2\, ln\left(POP_{j,t}\right) + \omega_3\, ln\left(FTA_{ij,t}\right) + \xi_{ij,t} \tag{1}$$

The FTA variable takes a value of 1 or 0, dependent on whether the countries *i* and *j* have an FTA between them or not, respectively. Then a distance variable is added to Equation (1) to get to Equation (2):

$$ln\left(Imports\ to\ EFTA_{ij,t}\right) = \omega_0 + \omega_1\, ln\left(GDP_{j,t}\right) + \omega_2\, ln\left(POP_{j,t}\right) + \omega_3\, ln\left(FTA_{ij,t}\right) + \omega_4\, ln\left(DIS\_GEO_{ij}\right) + \xi_{ij,t} \tag{2}$$

Then it continues with estimating imports to EFTA, thus returning to the trade flow estimated:

$$ln\left(Imports\ to\ EFTA_{ij,t}\right) = \omega_0 + \omega_1\, ln\left(GDP_{j,t}\right) + \omega_2\, ln\left(POP_{j,t}\right) + \omega_3\, ln\left(FTA_{ij,t}\right) + \xi_{ij,t} \tag{3}$$

At the end, imports to EFTA are estimated. The distance variable is added to Equation (3) to get to Equation (4):

$$ln\left(Imports\ to\ EFTA_{ij,t}\right) = \omega_0 + \omega_1\, ln\left(GDP_{j,t}\right) + \omega_2\, ln\left(POP_{j,t}\right) + \omega_3\, ln\left(FTA_{ij,t}\right) + \omega_4\, ln\left(DIS\_GEO_{ij}\right) + \zeta_{ij,t} \tag{4}$$

Then it continues with estimating exports from EFTA, thus returning to the trade flow estimated:

$$ln\left(Exports\ from\ EFTA_{ij,t}\right) = \omega_0 + \omega_1\, ln\left(GDP_{j,t}\right) + \omega_2\, ln\left(POP_{j,t}\right) + \omega_3\, ln\left(FTA_{ij,t}\right) + \varepsilon_{ij,t} \tag{5}$$

At the end, exports from EFTA are estimated. The Distance was added to Equation (5) to get to Equation (6):

$$ln\left(Exports\ from\ EFTA_{ij,t}\right) = \omega_0 + \omega_1\, ln\left(GDP_{j,t}\right) + \omega_2\, ln\left(POP_{j,t}\right) + \omega_3\, ln\left(FTA_{ij,t}\right) + \omega_4\, ln\left(DIS\_GEO_{ij}\right) + \varsigma_{ij,t} \tag{6}$$

Data

EFTA countries are Iceland, Liechtenstein, Norway, and Switzerland in the period analysed. We therefore included all these countries in the study, accounting for small remote economies (Kristjánsdóttir & Kristjánsdóttir, 2021; Kristjánsdóttir & Óskarsdóttir, 2021) except for Liechtenstein, since data for Liechtenstein is not available in the UN Comtrade Database (2021), in the OECD (OECD, 2020; Kristjánsdóttir & Karlsdóttir, 2020), or the World Bank (2021) databases; these databases provide interesting and unique comparison between countries on comparable bases.

The summary statistics for the basic data sample are presented in Table 1.2.

Table 1.1 Variable definition

EXP_iceland$_{j,t}$ EXP_china$_{j,t}$ EXP_norway$_{j,t}$ EXP_switzerland$_{j,t}$	Exports from the EFTA countries to China are as follows. Exports run over time and countries. Values are obtained from the following source: Trade Value (US$), UN Comtrade Database (2019) (https://comtrade.un.org/data/)
IMP_iceland$_{j,t}$ IMP_china$_{j,t}$ IMP_norway$_{j,t}$ IMP_switzerland$_{j,t}$	Imports to the EFTA countries from China are as follows. Imports run over time and countries. Values are obtained from the following source: Trade Value (US$), UN Comtrade Database (2019) (https://comtrade.un.org/data/)
Dist_iceland$_{j,t}$ Dist_china$_{j,t}$ Dist_norway$_{j,t}$ Dist_switzerland$_{j,}$	The regression is based on the weighted distance from Iceland, Norway, and Switzerland to China. Weighted distances obtained from SciencesPo http://econ.sciences-po.fr/thierry-mayer/data (2018). http://econ.sciences-po.fr/sites/default/files/file/tmayer/data/gravity.zip
FTA$_{it}$	The binary variable for FTA, taking the value of 1, if the countries' trade agreements are in place, and taking the value of 0 otherwise.

Table 1.2 Summary statistics for the basic sample, 2010–2017

Variable	*Obs*	*Mean*	*Std. Dev.*	*Min*	*Max*
LN(EXP_iceland$_{j,t}$)	1035	13,45878	3,639101	3,091042	22,40014
LN(EXP_china$_{j,t}$)	1697	20,30151	3,033706	7,445418	28,48215
LN(EXP_norway$_{j,t}$)	1652	15,82389	3,642307	5,442418	25,80437
LN(EXP_switzerland$_{j,t}$)	1793	16,94746	3,747211	2,302585	26,60353
LN(IMP_iceland$_{j,t}$)	1144	13,73125	3,735677	2,944439	22,66499
LN(IMP_china$_{j,t}$)	1555	18,55056	4,526548	2,197225	28,30358
LN(IMP_norway$_{j,t}$)	1487	15,4701	4,322456	4,812184	25,23174
LN(IMP_switzerland$_{j,t}$)	1678	16,45236	4,277296	3,135494	26,49486
LN(GDP$_{iceland,t}$)	8	23,54178	0,1945254	23,31182	23,89753

(Continued)

Table 1.2 (Continued)

Variable	*Obs*	*Mean*	*Std. Dev.*	*Min*	*Max*
$LN(GDP_{china,t})$	8	29,87048	0,2333976	29,43941	30,13554
$LN(GDP_{norway,t})$	8	26,82892	0,1399113	26,63967	26,98381
$LN(GBP_{switzerland,t})$	8	27,232	0,0599664	27,0928	27,28738
$LN(POO_{iceland,t})$	8	12,69761	0,0252743	12,66994	12,74047
$LN(POP_{china,t})$	8	21,03164	0,0124676	21,01422	21,04997
$LN(POP_{norway,t})$	8	15,44405	0,0271958	15,40255	15,47986
$LN(POP_{switzerland,t})$	8	15,91218	0,0277579	15,87282	15,95157

Table 1.2 presents the summary statistics for the Basic Sample, showing data running from the year 2010 through 2017. The exports/imports data run over the exporting country (i), importing country (j), over time (t), estimated in years. The obtained trade value (US$) is presented according to the UN Comtrade Database (2021). The distance data presented he weighted distances between countries. We obtain the weighted distances from SciencesPo (2019). The FTA is a binary variable for FTAs; taking the value of one (1) if the countries had a trade agreement in place and the value of zero (0) otherwise. As previously mentioned, Iceland and Switzerland had individual FTAs with China; Norway did not.

Regression results

Tables 1.3 and 1.4 present the linear regression results obtained for the sample.

The first column of Table 1.3 presents the regression results for import to the EFTA countries of Iceland, Norway, and Switzerland from China, during the time period 2010–2017. The *t* value presented in the table shows the significance of 10% 1.645, 5% 1.96, and 1% 2.58 for α 2-tailed tests. The results indicate that gross domestic product (GDP) significantly affects imports to the EFTA countries from China, with GDP having positive effects on imports to the EFTA countries from China. Population (POP) does not affect the amount of exports. Moreover, imports were found to be significantly affected by the FTAs coming into effect, indicating that the implementation of FTAs had positive effects on the trade flow in the form of imports from China. The second column of Table 1.3 indicates that when adding distance to the equation, distance has significant negative effect on imports. However, the FTA variable is no longer significant.

Table 1.4 shows the export from the EFTA countries of Iceland, Norway, and Switzerland, to China, 2010–2017. Table 1.4 first column results indicate that the population has significant positive effect on export from Iceland to China. It was found that the population effects were negative, but the GDP effects were positive, with the t value obtained. However, when considering the sign and size of the variable coefficients simultaneously, the economic and market size effects can be combined. Then the per capita effects are captured, indicating that the ln(GDP) - ln(POP) = ln(GDP/POP) values are found to have positive effects on exports from

Table 1.3 Import to Iceland, Norway, and Switzerland from China, 2010–2017

Regressors	*Equation (3)*	*Equation (4)*
	ln(*Imp to* $EFTA_{ij,t}$)	ln(*Imp to* $EFTA_{ij,t}$)
ln($GDP_{j,t}$)	1.056*** (3.91)	0.719** (2.56)
ln($POP_{j,t}$)	−0.133 (−0,42)	0.247 (0.76)
ln($FTA_{ij,t}$)	0.156* (−1.77)	−0.051 (−0.57)
ln (DIS_GEO_{ij})		−1.982** (−2.44)
Constant	−4.597* (−1.92)	16.429* (1.85)
R-sq	0.988	0.991
Observations	24	24

Robust t-statistics reported in parentheses. ***, **, * significant at the 1, 5, and 10 per cent levels, respectively.

Table 1.4 Exports from EFTA countries, Iceland, Norway, and Switzerland, to China, 2010–2017

Regressors	*Equation (5)*	*Equation (6)*
	ln(*Exp from* $EFTA_{ij,t}$)	ln(*Exp from* $EFTA_{ij,t}$)
In ($GDP_{j,t}$)	1.833*** (8.95)	0.666 (1.53)
In ($POP_{j,t}$)	−0.473*** (−3.06)	1.079** (2.14)
In ($FTA_{ij,t}$)	0.291 (0.99)	0.110 (0.78)
ln ($Distance_{ij}$)		11.673*** (9.21)
Constant	−19.136*** (−6.02)	−116.698*** (−8.43)
R-sq	0.944	0.992
Observations	31	24

Robust t-statistics reported in parentheses. ***, **, * significant at the 1, 5, and 10 per cent levels, respectively.

EFTA to China. This is because the resultant of ln(GDP) - ln(POP) has a positive sign, that is when presented as ln(GDP/POP). This is due to transformation when using the logarithm function. FTA was founded to have positive insignificant effects on exports from the EFTA to China. Table 1.4 second column results indicate that when the distance variable is added to the equation, distance does not negatively affect exports, and the FTA continues to have positive but insignificant effects on exports from the EFTA to China.

Summary and conclusions

The objective of this research is to analyse international trade relations between the EFTA trade bloc and China, along with FTAs with China since 2014. More specifically, we are interested in them if they are beneficial for the EFTA trade bloc to have FTAs with China. This is because there are individual countries within the European Free Trade Association (EFTA) that have FTAs with China. We use numerical presentations, and we present econometric analysis to investigate the impact on the EFTA countries. We use exports and imports for the investigation.

Main results obtained in this research are following. First, findings indicate that gross domestic product (GDP) has significant effect on imports to EFTA from China, as well as the presence of FTAs. Population (market size) was not confirmed to have effects on imports to EFTA; however, the FTAs do have a positive significant effect. Second, when testing for the effects of FTAs on exports from EFTA to China in a similar gravity model specification, it was found that FTAs have positive insignificant impacts on exports from the EFTA countries to China. At the end, the results taken together (for Tables 1.3 and 1.4) indicated that the FTAs were beneficial for imports to individual EFTA countries from China. However, FTAs were not estimated to have positive significant effects on exports from the EFTA countries to China in the period analysed. The conclusion is therefore that FTAs appear to be primarily beneficial for exports from China, since they positively affect imports to the EFTA countries from China. However, FTAs are not beneficial for exports from EFTA to China.

All in all, the results appear to be positive for exports from China, and not for exports to China - in other words, FTAs stimulate flow from China, not flow to China. Based on that, it appears as FTAs between the EFTA countries and China will not pay off for the European countries. However, this holds for the period analysed and needs to be carefully considered when analysing the impact on current and later developments.

2 Chinese investments in the Nordic digital platforms

Meelis Kitsing

Introduction

The Chinese Foreign Direct Investments (FDI) in Europe are increasingly being seen as a foundation for a long-term geopolitical strategy. This implies that the economic developments are interlinked with political and social aspects. European decision-makers increasingly associate FDI with "systemic rivalry" between the EU and China rather than with pure economic transactions (ECFR, 2020). The Nordic countries have been open to FDI and have the most advanced digital ecosystems in Europe, which have also benefited from the inflow of Chinese investments. At the same time, emerging political rhetoric in Europe emphasizes "technological sovereignty" and calls for "forceful decoupling" from China and strengthening "our sovereignty in strategic value chains" (Cerulus, 2020). Hence, the chapter explores restrictions on national level and explores Chinese investments in the Nordic digital platforms on a micro level. The Chinese FDI in the Nordic digital platforms is also conceptually challenging as these aforementioned public policy dilemmas insist that it cannot be tackled from the perspective of one discipline alone. The combination approaches of international relations and political economy with that of economics, particularly institutional economics focusing on transaction costs, provide a more comprehensive framework.

Particularly fundamental is the debate between neoliberals and neorealists in international relations, which comes down to the question of whether states are driven by absolute or relative gains in their interactions in the anarchic world (Baldwin, 1993). Cooney and Sato (2009) have astutely classified neorealists as seeing the world as a zero-sum conflict, meanwhile, neoliberals assert that cooperation rather than conflict is needed for prosperity. Neoliberals assert that states ought to be driven by the absolute gains, which results in absolute benefit for the states. Chinese FDI in Europe benefits both as they both gain in the absolute sense – Chinese firms expand in Europe, and Europeans get additional source of finance. Neorealists claim that the motive for states ought to be the relative gains, which implies the change in position vis-à-vis other states. Chinese digital platforms such as Tencent grow larger while Europe has no globally important digital platforms. This debate is directly related to the role of China and its influence in the world economy. By some estimates such as combining Gross Domestic

DOI: 10.4324/9781003274933-2

Product (GDP), net capital flows and trade, China already surpassed the United States in 2020 (Economist, 2021). However, International Monetary Fund (IMF) has calculated on the basis of nominal GDP in terms of the 2017 international dollars that US economy will be larger than Chinese economy until 2030 when China will take over (IMF, 2020). However, a forecast by Capital Economics (2021) shows that China's economy will peak at 87 per cent of US GDP in nominal terms by 2030, but then its total GDP will decrease relative to the US GDP.

The linear assumption about the increasing dominance of China's economy ignores the fact that it has been relatively easy to achieve rapid growth so far. Economic growth becomes more difficult as China has to move from the level of extensive growth to the intensive growth where human capital, social capital, intellectual property and ability to constantly innovate become a norm (Acemoglu & Robinson, 2019). Many countries have not managed to make such a transition. The Soviet Union is an example which after decades of rapid growth and industrialization got stuck in stagnation in the 1970s and eventually economic mismanagement was a crucial factor in its demise. Obviously, China is not the Soviet Union, and its economy is more flexible and decentralized. However, most developing countries have not made the transition by getting stuck in so-called "middle-income trap". This uncertainty over China's growth prospects does not imply that focus on relative gains will ease. As Brands and Beckley (2021) write, the main problem is that China is a declining power which is more likely to lead to a conflict than leading to the rise of China. They challenge conventional wisdom behind the Thucydides Trap where the China's rise increases the danger of war (Brands & Beckley, 2021). Instead, they draw on historical evidence to argue that usually increasing powers on their peak start to behave recklessly stemming from the uncertainty about their future. In a nutshell, If China's economy overtakes that of the United States, it will increase security concerns in the United States and among its allies leading to policy measures to restrict certain FDIs. If China's relative power declines vis-à-vis the United States, it creates additional motivation to subject such investments to political control from Beijing and accordingly restrict them in the West. All kinds of transaction costs and complexity associated with such investments will increase. North (1990) points out that the economic progress is dependent transaction costs. Restrictive rules of the game increase transaction costs which, in turn, hinder economic progress (North, 1990).

Transaction costs are fundamental for the economics of platforms, which reduce inefficiencies by exploiting network effects and economies of scale which often lead to winner-takes-it-all business model (Katz & Shapiro, 1994; Parker & van Alstyne, 2005; Noe & Parker, 2005; Kitsing, 2021). These fundamental elements combined by the exploitation of two-sided markets (Rochet & Tirole, 2006), multisided markets (Evans, 2003) as well as long-tail markets (Brynjolfsson et al., 2006) allow platforms to grow rapidly on a global scale. These are the reasons why Chinese platform business groups such as Tencent and Alibaba are eager to invest in digital platforms around the world. On the other hand, these are exactly the reasons why regulators will pay attention more to the Chinese digital platform investments. In a nutshell, a focus on relative gains implies more restrictive rules of the game concerning the Chinese FDI into Europe. Whether these general rules will increase transaction costs for digital platforms or not will be explored in the later parts of the chapter.

Comparison of FDI rules and Chinese investments

This comparison focuses on three countries and one digital platform in each country on the basis of secondary sources and insights from semi-structured interviews. In order to understand the FDI-related regulatory environment, a comparative analysis focuses on Estonia, Finland and Sweden. It highlights main rules concerning FDI screening. Even though all three countries are members of the EU where there is considerable harmonization on the rules concerning economic activities, the EU Screening Regulation (Regulation (EU) 2019/452) from March 2019 is "delicate and not harmonizing" (Magnusson, 2021). The EU Commission has offered guidance in March 2020 to the member states concerning foreign direct investment and free movement of capital from third countries and the protection of Europe's strategic assets, ahead of the application of FDI screening regulation. However, the most rules concerning FDI are still national.

The OECD FDI Regulatory Restrictiveness Index shows that Estonia and Finland are some of the least restrictive countries in the EU. Sweden is actually among more restrictive countries in the EU, but the general level of regulatory restrictiveness in the EU is very low – particularly in comparison with China which is, together with Russia, India and New Zealand, among some of the most restrictive countries. But the United States is also significantly more restrictive than the EU (OECD, 2020). Regulatory restrictions are also different. Estonia has primarily equity-related restrictions, while Finland has some equity restrictions but primarily other restrictions. Sweden has mainly equity and screening and approval restrictions (OECD, 2020).

In order to understand how these more general rules may affect FDI inflows into digital platform companies, Swedish health care platform Doktor.se, Finnish gaming platform Supercell and Estonian ride-sharing platform Bolt.ee are explored on the basis of document analysis and semi-structured interviews. All these companies have received investments from Chinese platform groups, but their business areas as well as political and social visibility and sensitivity are different. As Estonia, Finland and Sweden have some of the most digital ecosystems in the EU, the comparison of national rules as well as specific platforms serve as representative of other economies in Europe and are particularly relevant cases in exploring the potential trajectories for other European countries. The relevance does stem not only from the presence of advanced digital ecosystems and Chinese investments but also from a perspective of research methods. Essentially, they are extreme cases as the digitalization in many areas has advanced to highest level according to the Digital Economy and Society Index by the European Commission (2020). As Seawright (2016) has argued, extreme cases "are the best alternatives for a broad range of discovery-related goals". If certain patterns persist in these countries concerning Chinese FDIs despite regulations, then it is also highly probable that the same outcome will prevail in other EU countries as well.

Sweden and Doktor.se

Sweden has been an open country towards trade and FDI throughout decades. The concerns about Chinese investment have been smaller as in some other European countries. For instance, Chinese have taken over Volvo, a symbolic carmaker in Sweden for decades. Sweden has been known also in the European Union as a promoter of free trade and a sceptic of initiatives that lead to trade protection such as EU-wide digital tax. In recent years, there has been also quite a lot of changes in Sweden as overall business environment has changed considerably. Recently, investments have increased and diversified, and specific investment types such as venture capital has developed (Lindman, 2021). At the same time, new amendments have been made concerning FDI-screening to the Protective Security Act which entered into force on 1 January 2021. This fast-tracking initiative was particularly expedited by the COVID-19 pandemic. Furthermore, Swedish government has undertaken an investigation to propose legislation introducing a comprehensive FDI-screening procedure and blocking mandate. This inquiry is set to deliver its proposal in November 2021. However, these FDI-specific moves have not influenced the Chinese FDI into digital platforms in Sweden (Lindman, 2021). Rather, other regulations in more general way affect investments, including from China. Banks have an obligation to track and scrutinize transfers more than before and follow transaction rules on origin and destination of capital flows.

From music to healthcare

Sweden is home to Spotify which is the most popular audio streaming subscription service that gives users access to millions of songs and other content. While Spotify is a household name throughout the United States and Europe, it is a lesser known fact that one of the largest shareholders of Spotify is the Chinese digital platform Tencent. Tencent owned 9.1% of common stocks in Spotify in the summer of 2020 (Ingham, 2020). This investment has a rationale for global market sharing as Spotify has not entered into the Chinese market. At the same time, Tencent Music Entertainment (TME) dominates the Chinese market. In 2017, Spotify and TME agreed to a stock swap of their respective companies (Ma et al., 2017). Despite Spotify being the largest digital platform in Europe, music-sharing is not a politically sensitive field. However, changes in healthcare provision have much more political tensions. Political and other transaction costs lead to inefficiencies that digital platformization can potentially reduce. Healthcare space has seen a huge change in Sweden with a transformation of "very closed off system" to more open system and heavy investments from multiple sources, including venture capital (Lindman, 2021).

Tencent's investment in Doktor.se

Swedish platform Doctor.se is a large provider of digital healthcare with physical clinics in Sweden and digital services available in different countries of the world. The platform offers the services of nurses, general practitioners and specialist doctors through its telemedicine services which is often integrated with other service providers such as veterinary care chain AniCura in Europe, telecommunications group Proximus in Belgium and digital healthcare provider Vibe in Brazil. Since its inception in 2016, Doktor.se has seen rapid growth where, among its investors, has been the Chinese digital platform Tencent. In July 2021, the company announced that Tencent will invest up to 29.5 million euros in Doktor.se through issuing of new shares and buying shares from existing owners (Doktor.se, 2021). This investment follows earlier investment by Tencent, which increased their share in the platform to 5 per cent. Other large investors are two founders Doktor.se with 7.5 per cent and Finnish health and well-being corporation Oriola with 7 per cent, which diluted its ownership from previous 14 per cent in May 2021 (Oriola, 2021). Overall, Doktor.se has 300 investors who are entrepreneurs, including family offices and other private individuals from Sweden. It does not have a venture capital investment. As Doktor.se is widely used in Sweden by one tenth of Swedish population by some estimates and it carried out 1.2 million patient consultations either physically or digitally in 2020, the investments offer opportunities for international expansion.

Rationale for Tencent's investment

Martin Lindman, CEO of Doktor.se, emphasized that it was a conscious decision to attract Tencent as one of the investors. "This is a huge change for the company as big player with a broader international perspective and a stature in multiple markets decided to invest," Lindman said. According to Lindman, it was biggest investment they can attract, and there were no alternatives for this size of investment and none that really mattered. Lindman does not see Tencent solely as a Chinese firm as they have hundreds of investments in Europe but rather as a global company. This investment is particularly important as Doktor.se prepares for initial public offering (IPO) in Stockholm in 2022. This also means that there will be new investors from all over the world, and company does not have control over who is investing. This investment does not affect Doktor.se, and what they do as 5 per cent stake is relatively small and does not give any control to Tencent. Prior to the decision, Doktor.se had a discussion on the board level, and they expected some concerns from stakeholders. However, benefits outweighed the potential risks (Lindman, 2021).

Nevertheless, investment received special attention and scrutiny in Sweden. "Discussion about it was more massive than expected," Lindman said. First, the doctors' union felt concerned about patient information. "They thought personal data will be handled by Chinese government. However, Tencent does not have control and access to data. Furthermore, it is illegal bounded by law and abusers can be sentenced to jail," pointed out Lindman. Second, this decision sparked a bigger conversation in Sweden whether Doktor.se as a Swedish company should accept money from country such as China. "This debate is a way above Doktor.se as it is difficult to make a distinction. Market is open and there are no rules and regulations against it. Various funds flow across the globe," said Lindman. The concerns about Tencent's investment spiked immediately when it was announced but decreased gradually after that. However, Lindman recognizes a potential risk associated with the investment. Even if Tencent's investment is not large, Doktor.se could be valued less if there are concerns about Tencent and Chinese platforms. However, such indirect setbacks can come through different channels and platforms can operate in a global economy. According to Lindman, Tencent ownership is not so important because it does not own majority stake. The investment is based on market terms and is a typical to investment of funds in Europe. Both parties had done good job in diligence before the investment was done (Lindman, 2021).

Doktor.se is also in the middle of discussions whether to expand to China and other Asian markets. "We are looking at entire global market now in addition to 7 countries such as Brazil and Belgium where we already operate," says Lindman. In Lindam's view, next 10 years can see frictions in the world economy and restrictions on the flow of capital based on attitudes "we don't want your money". But he argues that it would be difficult to implement in practice because many of these companies are so international. "Where do you draw the line?" Lindman asks. "There is Middle- East money, Russian money, political tensions and frictions but it is a long way that we can control the capital flows but there will be some control," he adds.

Finland and Supercell

Finland has been open to FDI throughout the decades as the OECD index shows, but some restrictions have been in place since 2012 such as the act on the Monitoring of Foreign Corporate Acquisitions. The last amendments were made to the act in 2020. The Ministry of Economic Affairs and Employment is responsible for implementation. Foreign owner is a foreign national or legal entity not established within the EU and EFTA countries. The latter includes Iceland, Liechtenstein, Norway and Switzerland. If the foreign owner owns more than 10 per cent in legal entity in the EU and EFTA countries, it will be also subject to the act. Finnish government plans to expand the scope of application of FDI screening related to functions vital to society and issues of national security, authorities' resources and foreign and security policy objectives. This is particularly driven by the changes in the international security environment and diversity of security threats. The COVID-19 pandemic has speeded up these developments. The plan is to establish different ownership thresholds at 10 per cent, 30 per cent and 50 per cent, respectively (Magnusson, 2021).

The Ministry of Economic Affairs and Employment can scrutinize cases also at their will. Usually, the defence industry and providers of goods and services to Finnish authorities are assumed to be the main subject of the FDI screening. However, the law does not specify which companies and industry are subject to monitoring. The assessment of threats to national security is time- and case-specific. If the investment is not approved, the foreign owner must dispose of ownership or there are limitations set on company control through restrictions on voting rights. So far, the main issue has been the acquisition of real estate and land, particularly by Russians, and not the acquisition of digital platforms. There have been cases of Finnish islands being owned by Russian-government-related interests where the Ministry of Defence approval is also required now, and municipal authorities often consult with the ministry in advance of planned real estate transactions. In fact, Finnish expert Mikko Hüpponen from F-Secure has pointed out that cybersecurity often takes a back seat. There are increasingly more cyberattacks from China, but many government agencies say that they do not have mandate for dealing with cybersecurity (Hüpponen, 2021). The restrictions concerning investments to Finnish digital platforms do not stem from FDI screening but are more likely related to general business and employment regulations. For instance, Estonian ride-sharing platform Bolt and Uber both tried to operate initially in Helsinki but soon closed down their operations because of protectionist legislation. Many leading digital platform founders such as Peter Vesterbacka of Rovio which created Angry Boards particularly complain about the Finnish immigration authorities, which make processing of work visas for technology entrepreneurs difficult and time-consuming (Vesterbacka, 2021). Hired workers often have to wait for 12–18 months for processing their work permits. Technology entrepreneur Petri Kajander points out that Sweden has a lot of tech investment in data farms because Finnish regulations are not favourable. “In this sense, Finland is not good place for technology investments and developing new business models because of its conservatism and trade unions,” says Kajander. “Finland has a strong status quo preference combined with technology resistance and incompetence. It is a platform of denial. Restrictions are not China specific,” adds Kajander. For instance, Finnish authorities have filed criminal charges for financial crimes against Antero Vartia, a former Green Party MP and founder of non-profit platform Wecompensate, which aims to offset carbon footprint. The case seems to be about offering tips (monetary reward) for environmentally friendly behaviour (Hämäläinen, 2021). Similarly, Finnish food delivery unicorn Wolt, which was acquired by DoorDash for 8.1 billion US dollars in November 2021, is scrutinized at its home market because of a legal case filed by Finnish trade union PAM about the employment status of its couriers (Keane, 2021).

Tencent's investment in Supercell

Tencent has also acquired many gaming firms over the years as the gaming platforms have been one of its focus areas in China and abroad (see Chapter 7 in this book for a broader perspective). In 2016, Tencent was part of Luxembourg consortium which acquired an 81.4 per cent stake of the Finnish mobile game maker called Supercell at the valuation of 10.2 billion dollars. Supercell is known for creating the acclaimed "Clash of Clans". In October 2019, Tencent spent additional 40 million dollars to increase its share in the consortium from 50 per cent to 51.2 per cent (Perez, 2019). However, this investment must be seen in its broader context and not as a particular investment targeted towards Finland (Kajander, 2021). Rather, it is a result of a vibrant gaming industry in the ecosystem Helsinki. In Finland, this investment is not being seen as strategic and related to national security. In many ways, gaming is a niche affair and takes place primarily in the virtual space. Tencent's initial investment happened because Softbank, a large Japanese investor in Supercell, decided to exit from Supercell. In 2013, Softbank purchased 51 per cent stake in Supercell at the valuation of 1.5 billion dollars. "Initially, Softbank's investment into Supercell was shown as a big deal. They promised to commit for 150–200 years, pay taxes in Finland, keep Supercell's headquarters in Helsinki," says Kajander. "Apparently, they needed money for another investment and sold Supercell to Tencent," he adds. The valuation in 2013 meant that Softbank's share was worth about 770 million, while for exit in 2016 such stake had increased to over 5 billion. According to Kajander, Supercell was looking for an amicable long-term investor. They tried to avoid European and US competitors and found an investor which was not directly competing. Supercell is a private company, and hence many details concerning the investment are not public. One founder Ilkka Paananen stayed on as the CEO, and another founder left Supercell. Their headquarters remained in Helsinki. Supercell has paid considerable amount of taxes in Finland which were often heavier than other industries. They have contributed to creating a positive image of Finland to be the best ecosystem for gaming companies in the world. Considering all of this gaming is not really a critical issue concerning Chinese FDI. For instance, the planned tunnel between Helsinki and Tallinn championed by technology entrepreneur Peter Vesterbacka has received much more attention concerning Chinese investments as they are being seen as one option for financing the project (Kajander, 2021). According to Kajander, it is not likely that significant restrictions will be imposed on Chinese investments into digital platforms. "Restrictions are more about Russia. Even the tunnel between Helsinki and Tallinn is not so much about China but about internal politics of Helsinki city where China is used as an excuse," says Kajander.

Estonia and Bolt

Estonia has had very open FDI regime throughout the last three decades. The main reasons for limiting FDI are related to real estate and national defence. So far Estonia has not sent any notifications to European Commission on planned changes to the FDI – differently from Latvia and Lithuania which have done so. However, the government is conducting a study for potentially new FDI screening regime (Magnusson, 2021).

However, the main concerns in Estonia do not come from general rules but rather from specific cases. Differently from Finland and Sweden, Estonia belongs to the North Atlantic Treaty Organisation (NATO). For Estonian government, security cooperation with the United States is crucial element not only in its defence and foreign policy but increasingly in its technology policy as well. In this sense, the US interests often define Estonian interests. Estonia has gone further than many other European governments to implement restrictions concerning non-EU companies' equipment use in the development of 5G network (ERR, 2020).

This implies that one network provider Elisa, a Finnish telecom company, has to replace the Huawei network equipment in the coming years with an estimated cost of half billion euros (ERR, 2020). However, the Estonian government and Elisa disagree on compensation. Elisa is willing to do it in a shorter time frame as long as investments will be compensated by the Estonian government, while Estonian government is accepting a longer time frame for the technology replacement as long as it does not have to be compensated. However, this is a specific case stemming from the US interests concerning Huawei and China. Most importantly, the case cannot be generalized to other digital platforms in Estonia.

Didi's investment in Bolt

In 2017, Didi Chuxing, the largest ride-sharing company in China backed by both Tencent and Alibaba, invested in Estonian ride-sharing company Bolt (at that time it was called Taxify). The sum of this investment is undisclosed, but Bolt announced during the formation of partnership that "DiDi will invest in and collaborate with us to support our further growth and innovation across all markets" (Bolt, 2017). In August 2021, Bolt was valued over 4 billion US euros after raising 600 million euros from Sequoia Capital. In previous rounds, Bolt raised 110 million dollars from Naya Capital and 20 million euros from the International Financial Corporation of the World Bank. Other important investors have been German carmaker Daimler with 175 million dollars and European Investment Bank with 50 million euros. Bolt operates in more than 300 cities and 45 countries across Europe, Asia, Latin America and Africa.

The COVID-19 pandemic led to 75 per cent drop in Bolt's revenues, but the ride-sharing platforms were able to continue operations without layoffs and attract new investments in the middle of COVID-19. Despite these developments, Didi decided to exit from Bolt and sold a stake in Spring 2021, which, at its highest point, was 13 per cent of the total shares of Bolt (Estonian Business Registry, 2021). Obviously, Bolt benefited from having access to Didi's network of knowledge and experience as Didi had invested in ride-hailing apps around the globe, which are often the competitors of Uber. "Probably also it was Didi's decision and their strategy rather than Estonian investment climate, concerns about China and Bolt which led to the exit," pointed out Kajander. "There is a lot of internal politics in China which has put a lot of pressure on entrepreneurs, all kind of travel and investment restrictions may affect them," he added (Kajander, 2021). The complexity makes it difficult to understand the incentives for the exit by Didi. It could be pure business decision or could be motivated by Chinese politics to a greater or lesser extent. Nevertheless, it does not have probably to do with Bolt and Estonia being of strategic importance for Chinese FDI.

Discussion and conclusion

Chinese FDI has been flowing increasingly into the different sectors of European economy and is in a high place in the radar screen of politicians. The US government has increasingly started to scrutinize Chinese investments which had partially spilled over to the European Union as well and naturally contributed to the tensions between China and the United States. These developments have led to new rulemaking on European and national levels.

However, these FDI-screening rules are still left primarily to national governments which have followed diverse approaches so far. The comparison of Estonia, Finland and Sweden demonstrated this regulatory diversity. Most importantly, these new rules and associated political rhetoric have not affected three digital platforms studied in this chapter. The FDI restrictions focus on more traditional transactions such as real estate.

In general, Estonia and Finland have less-restrictive FDI-screening rules than Sweden. But in all cases, these rules do not create barriers for Chinese investments into digital platforms in these countries. Barriers are either created by other regulations concerning employment as in Finland, social attitudes as in Sweden concerning data and ethical issues in Chinese investments and specific security and foreign policy commitments as in Estonia due to the NATO membership and commitment to follow US interests.

In all three platforms studied, barriers for Chinese FDI were not considerable. Rather, it was the opposite. Concerns about the health care data were unfounded in the case of Doktor.se because as a minority investor Tencent has no control of company and no access to data. Even though Tencent is a majority owner of Supercell, the gaming company is not considered to be a strategic asset and vital for national security. Even though Bolt is politically and socially most visible of Estonian unicorns because of immigrant workers, issues with electric scooters and car rental made easy, Didi's stake in Bolt and exit from Bolt did not receive similar levels of public attention as numerous other issues. In many ways, Chinese investments into digital platforms are a no issue. Particularly so, as it was a minority stake approaching 13 per cent of total share at its highest. It is plausible that technology entrepreneurs underestimate the effects of regulatory tightening in the future. The Chinese platforms certainly underestimated their government's regulatory onslaught as the cases of Alibaba and Ant Financial demonstrate. However, the EU and its members' states are democratic countries where rulemaking takes time – even if the political rhetoric concerning Chinese FDI has heated up. Regulatory complexity leads also to regulatory arbitrage and unintended consequences which policymakers do not often foresee. Regulatory uncertainty is likely to increase transaction costs which are handled better by large platforms with significant resources rather than small players. As the road to hell is paved with good intentions, the regulatory tightening may end up being favourable for large global players and may create barriers for future platform entrepreneurs from Europe.

3 Japanese trade in services and FDI in Europe

Evidence from Estonia

Riina Kerner

Introduction

The chapter compares the main findings from the Japanese and Estonian services' trade and foreign direct investment (FDI) analysis showing that Estonian exports to Japan and FDI inward flows from Japan were almost equal in 2020 (28 versus 24 million euros), which was not the case before COVID-19 pandemic, when the services' exports were twofold larger than FDI. Many theoretical discussions treat all FDIs and service exports as alternative ways of serving a foreign market. Thus, this chapter presents the patterns of FDI and services' trade in Japan and Estonia in 2010–2020 with the influences of the COVID-19 outbreak, looking at a handful of other countries (including Latvia, Lithuania and Finland). The data is derived from the Balance of Payments surveys that are in charge of national central banks, thus obtaining service trade with investment indicators and some indexes. Estonia attracts investments with a business-friendly environment and exports knowledge-intensive services abroad, including Japan. At the same time, Japan, on the contrary, invests a lot in abroad countries, including Estonia. As a result, trade and investments bring valuable benefits to both countries, including jobs and the movement of companies.

The gravity model explains why the flows between Estonia and Japan are assumed low – Estonian economy is small (in the numerator), and the distance between two countries is 7800 km (hence, large number in the denominator). Furthermore, it is confirmed also that the FDI (capital) itself is accompanied by the transfer of technological know-how and knowledge in international markets. According to the gravity model, small FDI flows between Estonia and Japan were assumed due to the differences in the size of the economy and 7800-kilometre distance between the two countries. Furthermore, it is confirmed also that service trade restrictions negatively impact the service trade and FDI flows and show a solid correlation between FDI and service trade per capita. Therefore, it recommends that analysing service trade together with FDI inflows and outflows, which means also that country's "service trade balance", should be calculated as the net of "exports of services plus investment inflows" and "imports of services plus investment outflows". The results contribute to service trade and FDI

DOI: 10.4324/9781003274933-3

methodology development while analysing the flows from an Estonian perspective vis-a-vis Japan. This new methodological approach is essential for decision-makers, trade negotiators, and researchers. In 2021, Estonia celebrated the 100 years of friendship between Japan and Estonia, acknowledging that cultural factors and experiences are essential in expanding the trade relations between the countries. However, trade relations often have been considered challenging due to the specific legal and non-legal requirements.

Foreign investors adjust their decision to trade or invest according to the investment environment and the characteristics of the economy. In the European Union, free movement of services and capital (investment) has been set up as the principle of the standard market system. Therefore, FDI and service flows of Estonia and Japan are analysed in conjunction with the size of the economy. In contrast, theoretically, flows are more intense between similar countries due to the size of the economy and neighbourhood or geography. Estonia is a technologically advanced small Nordic country with one of the smallest economies in the European Union, located between Latvia and Russia. Compared to Japan, Estonia is eight times smaller in terms of territory and 100 times in terms of population. Estonian GDP per capita is 60% of that of Japan's (24 thousand and 40 thousand, respectively[1]). The problem to be considered is the difference between Estonian and Japanese investing and trading behaviour. Estonia attracts investment, while Japan invests itself outside. As a result, Estonian investment inflows ratio to GDP was 9.8% in 2019, and the same for Japan was only 0.3%. The same measure in Latvia and Lithuania was 2%,[2] similar to the world average. Given those differences, we ask why the Estonian and Japanese services trading and investment are so different and the determinants of those differences. In this chapter, three directions explain the investment and trading pattern differences in Estonia and Japan: (1) The used service trade and investment methodology and the world trends; (2) the comparison of the bilateral flows between Estonia and Japan; and (3) the relationship and descriptive indicators between Estonia and Japan compared to the sample of 67 countries. They have contributed to the evidence-based analysis that shows that service trading should be analysed together with investing and enhancing service exports. The analysis of this data showed that service trade is more influenced by COVID-19 pandemic than all FDIs, one reason being also the large share of tourism-related services in service trade, which were hit the most. However, in economies where FDI is concentrated in tourism, contractions were severe also in FDI (UNCTAD, 2021a). Study results show that service trade is more influenced by distance and the global downturns than investment. The importance of this analysis is that service trade is analysed together with investment flows, however, often presented and often analysed separately. The quantitative and qualitative methods were used, and knowledge was derived from the recent studies' results and literature overview and the author′s experience on developing international service trade methodology statistics, particularly for service trade by modes of supply (Rueda-Cantuche et al., 2016; Eurostat, 2017), while working in Eurostat, Statistical office of European Union.

Methodology of the study

Trading in services means that firms export and import (sell and purchase from abroad) services. Service trade means that intangible product is transferred to the foreign customer by different ways. Given the growing importance of services for economists and trade negotiators, the availability of service analysis is also decided by how they are supplied to the foreign customer. In this study, we also include the investment to deliver service abroad and enhance FDI-driven service trade, considering this as the mode, namely "commercial presence", abroad. Several methodological handbooks globally identify trade-in-services, but the main principles are covered by the general agreement on trade-in-services (GATS) (WTO, 1995), which splits services by four modes of supply indicating where and in which way service is supplied to foreign customers – mode 1: cross-border supply of services, that is from the territory of one country into the territory of another country; mode 2: consumption abroad, that is in the territory of one country to the consumers of another country; mode 3: commercial presence, that is by a service supplier of one country through establishment in the territory of another country; mode 4: presence of natural persons, that is by a service supplier of one country through the presence of natural persons in the territory of another country. For example computer services may be provided to the customer electronically (mode 1); through an affiliate abroad (FDI-driven or mode 3); through the presence of the person abroad (mode 4) or the presence of the customer in the home country (mode 2) (Figure 3.1) (Wettstein et al., 2019; Rueda-Cantuche et al., 2016). The limitation of this study is that services that are embedded in exported goods (e.g. software included in the mobile phone) were excluded, as

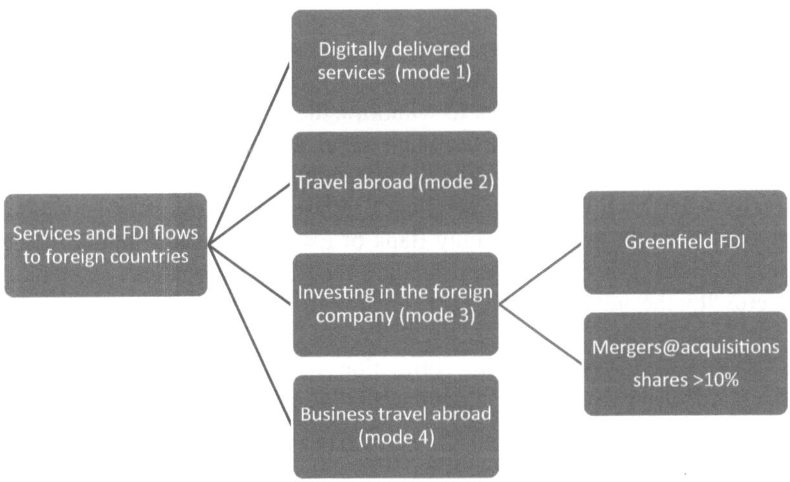

Figure 3.1 Services and FDI flows serving foreign markets (simplified)

Source: Based on WTO services mode of supply classification, author's elaboration.

those services are not captured by the GATS. These type of services might be considered as services supply through "mode 5" (Cernat & Kutlina-Dimitrova, 2014). However, this is a topic for further debate and analysis (Cernat, 2021). Together with trade-in-services, "money "can flow across borders of the countries also by foreign direct investment (FDI) flows. FDI flows accumulate in the economies finally as the foreign stocks of investment; however, this is not the scope of this chapter. Foreign direct investment (FDI) is a form of international capital flows, while foreign investors acquire some control over the other country's firm. The ownership of 10% or more of the voting power of a direct investment enterprise by a direct investor is evidence of a long-term relationship. Two main types of FDI are at focus in this chapter, as they are important from the market-entry perspective: (1) greenfield investment or direct investment in new facilities and (2) cross-border mergers and acquisitions.

FDI inward flows (or inflows) are capital flows invested into the company located in the hosting country. FDI outward flows (or outflows) are the capital flows that are funded outside the home country. FDI is a part of cross-border investment. An investor resident in one country establishes a lasting interest in another country with a significant influence over an enterprise. They can play a role in enhancing economic growth and creating jobs in the receiving economy. Moreover, the level of FDI may also indicate a particular attractiveness or competitiveness of an economy.

Financial transactions as flows between the direct investor and the direct investment enterprise are estimated by the Balance of Payments framework and the national banks compile data. Thus, FDI flows are transactions that are recorded during the reference period. However, world-level, recorded FDI inflows may not be equal to recorded FDI outflows due to imperfect geographic coverage, estimations and cross-country differences in compilation methods (UNCTAD, 2020).

FDI includes three elements: equity capital, reinvested earnings and intra-company loans. The negative flows may occur if any elements are negative – for example, when the bank decides to withdraw the investment from the country. The analysis was performed on the country level. The most recent publicly available data was used, mainly from years 2019 to 2020. The public databases from WTO, UNCTAD, OECD, CIA, Estonian Statistics, and Estonian Central Bank were used. For FDI, we used mainly Bank of Estonia data, benchmarking them against Eurostat data. Some negative values for FDI inflows have been replaced by "zeros "by the author". Estonia and Japan were compared not only bilaterally but also in conjunction with other countries. For comparative analysis, descriptive statistics were used, including correlation. In addition, the mirror data were used, regarding missing values, assuming that Japanese exports to Estonia equal Estonian imports from Japan. Knowledge-intensive services include telecommunication, computer, and information services and indicate the technological level of the economy. Services represent a large share of domestic activities. Still, they are currently less traded than goods due to the trade barriers, also suggested by the service trade restrictiveness measures listed by the World Bank and World

Trade Organization.[3] Therefore, in the analysis, following three indexes have been used:

(1) Service Trade Restrictiveness Index (STRI)[4] shows how open or closed the service market is to service suppliers. The index ranges from 0 to 100, with no restrictions to wholly completed to foreign services scale.
(2) Foreign Direct Investment Restrictiveness Index (Organization for Economic Co-operation and Development) measures restrictions on foreign direct investment across 22 economic sectors. Restrictions are evaluated on a 0 (open) to 1 (closed) scale.
(3) Ease of Doing Business Index[5] measures business regulations across economies. The scores range from 0 to 100 with higher scores indicating better business environments. The "trading" score shows how easy it is for companies to engage in international trade.

A gravity model for bilateral trade and FDI

By economic theory, open market and investment environment are effective measures to attract investment. But, for comparing two different countries Estonia and Japan in geography (7800 km distance between each other), size of population, territory, and economy, the gravity model predicts the bilateral trade flows that tend to fall with distance (Markusen & Venables, 1998). In the numerator of the fraction in the gravity model, the product of the size of the economies is registered, small for Estonia and large for Japan (GDP per capita 24 thousand and 40 thousand, respectively). In the denominator, the distance between two countries, 7800 km between Tallinn and Tokyo, is registered. Thus, the denominator being large, and one of the values being smaller in the product of the numerator, insignificant flows between Japan and Estonia are therefore assumed theoretically as well. However, the basic gravity model does not take into account the barriers and restrictions of trade as the determinants of trading or investing decisions (Talamo, 2007; La Porta et al., 1997) and openness to FDI flows (Shatz, 2000; Brenton & Manzocchi, 2002).

The primary gravity model states that bilateral flows between *country i and country j* are directly related to the product of the countries' GDP (*Yi* and *Yj*) and inversely related to their distance (*Dij*):

(1) $Fij = A * Yi * Yj / Dij$

where
Fij denotes flows (trade, FDI) between the home country *i* and the host country *j*,
A is a constant of proportionality,
Yi and *Yj* are economic sizes (GDP per capita) of countries *i* and *j*,
Dij denotes the distance between countries' capitals.

For analysing bilateral trade flows, a simple gravity model was used already by Tinbergen (1962). Since then, the gravity equation has also been applied to flows of capital. Furthermore, variables such as languages, culture, trade agreements, and law systems were added to the model (Mátyás, 1998; Cheng & Wall, 2004; Egger, 2000). Recently, WTO developed a gravity equation to predict the service trade flows by supply mode for countries with no data available (Wettstein et al., 2019). Thus, based on the gravity model, we may assume that bilateral flows between Japan and Estonia are pretty marginal due to the long distance between the two countries, differences in the size, and GDP per capita. The impact of political measures (barriers) has been relatively underexplored in the literature with some evidence on the service trade barriers that may affect the trading behaviour (Antràs & De Gortari, 2020; Benkovskis, 2019).

Empirical analysis

Service trade and FDI in the post-COVID world

The COVID-19 pandemic severely impacted global GDP and volume of goods and services exports, which declined in 2021 by 3% and 8%, respectively (Kutlina-Dimitrova, 2021), while services dropped by 20% (Figure 3.2). In 2016, service exports started to increase significantly, fourfold larger than FDI inflows in 2019, showing the growing importance of trading with services. However, due to the pandemic, tourism-related services dropped the most. Furthermore, in addition to the drop in service trade, COVID-related disruptions have also influenced the trade structure, with cross-border services flows becoming more relevant. New digitalization tools have further enhanced the service trade (e.g. conference platforms, e-mails, etc.), replacing supply modes (Cernat, 2021). However,

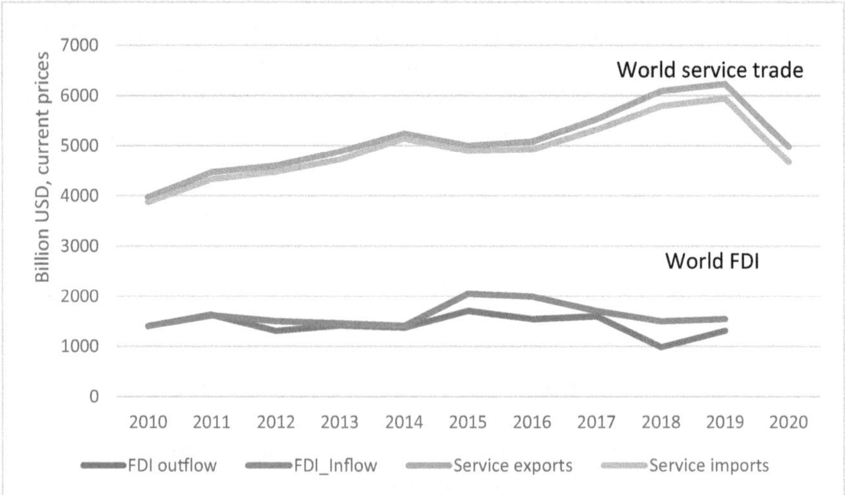

Figure 3.2 World FDI and service trade flows, USD, current prices 2010–2020

Source: UNCTAD services and FDI linked databases, 2021, accessed 05.10.2021.

post-COVID globalization has brought along new direct and indirect restrictive measures as well (closing borders and flights), hampering trade and investments for foreigners.

On the other hand, FDI flows remained on the same level, fluctuating annually between one and two trillion USD (Figure 3.2) during the last 15 years. FDI inflows dropped by one-third in 2020, falling to one trillion USD, which is lower than FDI inflows after the global financial crisis a decade ago (UNCTAD, 2021a). However, FDI inflows showed a downward trend already before the COVID-19 crisis. After having a peak of 2 trillion in 2015, the flows started to show downward trends as of 2016 (Figure 3.2).

COVID-19 has brought service supply closer to home; companies aim to gain from the proximity of the supplier and customer (Antràs & De Gortari, 2020). Thus, nearshoring matters more than offshoring. Production location decisions are important to consider for improving supply chain resilience during the pandemic times, and decisions to produce closer to the costumer may matter more than overseas, thus "nearshoring" instead of "offshoring" is preferred. Regarding policy measures, trends towards more restrictive measures affecting FDI accelerated in 2020. Of the 152 new investment policy measures adopted, 50 were designed to introduce new regulations or restrictions (UNCTAD, 2021a).

Service trade and FDI between Estonia and Japan

Estonia is considered attractive for FDI inflows, comprising 9.8% of GDP; on the contrary, in Japan, the same indicator is 0.3% (UNCTAD) (Table 3.1), and Japan is considered to have one of the most significant FDI outflows (UNCTAD). Therefore, this study focuses on bilateral flows between Estonia and Japan (not the countries' total flows). Estonia attracts investments from abroad, being among the leading countries in central and eastern Europe regarding FDI per capita. In 2020, the main countries investing in Estonia were Sweden and Finland, comprising 21% of the total FDI flows, followed by Luxembourgish (10%) and Dutch (6%) companies.[6] Due to the geography and scale differences, Japan's share was relatively negligible, less than 1% of Estonian investments until 2015. However, as of 2016, investments from Japan[7] had reached the share of 1.4% of Estonian

Table 3.1 Ratio of FDI to gross domestic product (GDP), 2019

Country	*InwardFlows*	*Outward Flow*
Estonia	9.79	6.33
Finland	3.05	1.71
Japan	0.29	4.45
Latvia	2.30	−0.47
Lithuania	1.81	0.28

Source: Data retrieved from UNCTAD report 2019.

total inward FDI (Figure 3.3). Similar shares were valid for services exported to Japan, reaching 0.8% of total service exports in 2019. But, for example, in Finland, the services exports to Japan comprised 3–4% (Figure 3.4).

In 2020, Estonian service exports to Japan have increased by sixfold compared to 2010, from 5 to 29 million euros (Figure 3.5, Table 3.2), peaking in 2019 with

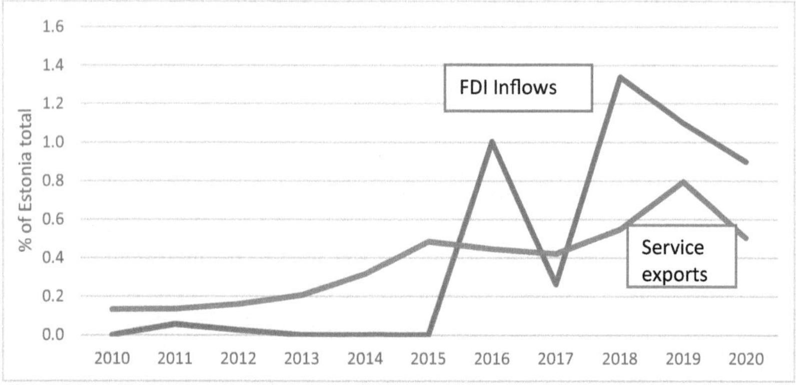

Figure 3.3 Share of Japan in Estonian service exports and FDI inflows, 2010–2020

Source: Data retrieved from Bank of Estonia and Statistics Estonia, 2010–2020.

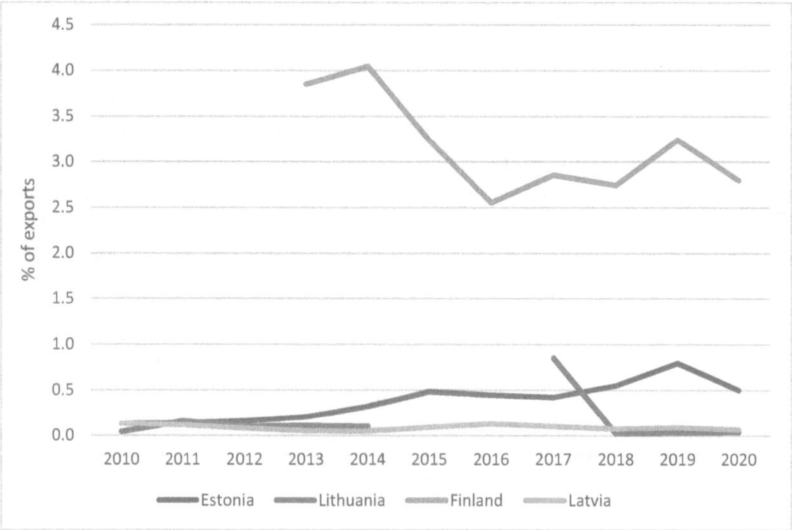

Figure 3.4 Japan's share in service exports from Estonian neighbourhood countries, 2010–2020

Source: Data retrieved from Eurostat, accessed 05.09.2021. Author´s calculations; breaks in series due to the confidentiality.

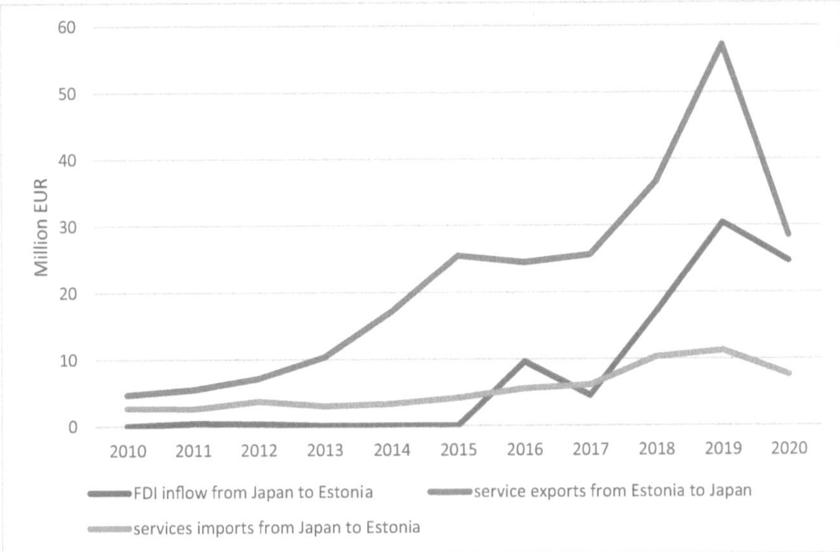

Figure 3.5 Estonian service trade and FDI inflows with Japan, in million euros, 2010–2020

Source: Data are retrieved from Bank of Estonia; Statistics Estonia, Eurostat, accessed 05.09.2021.

Table 3.2 FDI and service trade between Japan and Estonia, million euros, 2010–2020

	(1) FDI Inflow from Japan to Estonia	*(2) Service Exports from Estonia to Japan*	*(3) Services Imported from Japan*	*(4) FDI Outflow from Estonia to Japan*	*(5) Balance = (1+2) – (3+4)*
2010	0.00	4.70	2.70	0.00	2.00
2011	0.40	5.50	2.60	0	3.30
2012	0.30	7.10	3.70	0	3.70
2013	−0.6	10.3	3.0	NA	6.7
2014	−0.1	17.1	3.3	0	13.7
2015	0	25.5	4.2	0	21.3
2016	9.6	24.5	5.6	0	28.5
2017	4.5	25.6	6.1	NA	24.0
2018	17	36.5	10.3	NA	43.2
2019	30.4	57.1	11.2	NA	76.3
2020	24.7	28.5	7.6	NA	45.6

Source: Data retrieved from Bank of Estonia; Statistics Estonia, Eurostat. Accessed 05.09.2021, NA is “not available”.

57 million euros. Services exports from Estonia to Japan declined by twofold in 2020 compared to 2019 (from 57 to 29 million euros) (Table 3.2) and also due to the steep decrease in travel services, as tourism was hit the most in the COVID-19 crisis. On the other hand, FDI inflows to Estonia from Japan have been quite a recent trend, starting with 10 million euros in 2016 with the threefold increase by 2020. The inflows peaked at 30 million euros in 2019. Currently, FDI inflows and services exports are on the same level (25 and 29 million euros, respectively). Evidence showed that service exports have been more vulnerable to global outbreaks than FDI (Figure 3.3, Figure 3.4).

For considering whether the country is a net "winner" or "loser", the balance should be calculated based on both FDI and service trade (Table 3.2). Based on methodology (WTO, 1995) and further elaborations, we propose to use the following balance calculation: "services exports *plus* FDI inflows" (in both cases, money is received by the same economy) *minus* "service imports *plus* FDI outflows" (money is transferred abroad) (2). The integration of service trade and FDI flows may reduce part of methodological asymmetries in the services and FDI flows, as well as gives a better picture of the internationalization activities between the trading countries:

(1) (Service exports*ij* + FDI inflows*ij*) – (Service imports*ij* + FDI outflows*ij*) = Balance*ij*

where *i* is reporting country, and *j* is partner country.

The reasoning is derived from the GATS and *Manual on Statistics of International Trade in Services* (MSITS, United Nations, 2012) methodology; service trade and FDI have become inextricably intertwined. Therefore, FDI has a spillover effect, especially over service trade, with a strong correlation between FDI inflows per capita and service trade per capita (0.94). Furthermore, a strong correlation shows that FDI may cause the growth in FDI-related services (franchises, intellectual property, legal and accounting services, etc.). However, these causal effects are not investigated in this study. Therefore, as some countries are more investment-oriented (Japan), and others are more service-trade-(Estonia) oriented, we propose the new indicator to capture services and investment flows (as mode 3 in GATS) together.

The two countries, Estonia and Japan, have different cultural backgrounds. In addition, they are 7800 km apart from each other, but, nevertheless, the investors are ready to investigate the markets and invest and trade in services, regardless of the differences. As an example of developing a good partnership between Estonia and Japan, the Estonian Japan Trading Company (EJTC) was founded in Estonia some years ago, with a mission to create different investment lines between Estonia (and also the Baltic region) and Japan. This makes it easier for Estonian companies to establish themselves in the Japanese market. The supervisory board member of the company is a former sumo wrestler Kaido Höövelson, the most well-known Estonian in Japan. It is noteworthy to mention that the large shareholder of the EJTC is the Japanese company MBK Co. which is listed also in the

Tokyo Stock Exchange. Estonia is world-known for its e-governance solutions and start-up mentality; it is well located and positioned among knowledge-intensive companies and technologically advanced unicorns. Therefore, Estonian mindset with Japanese experience could be the formula for a successful partnership, in particular, on digital solutions and e-services, namely "X-road "in Estonia. Thus, based on the technological know-how, Estonian exports of knowledge-intensive services (information, computer services) could be an essential export "service article" and an opportunity to Japan. ICT services exports already comprised more than 10 per cent of Estonian services exports to Japan (Figure 3.6), explaining that Estonian ICT companies have discovered Japan as a potential destination country for ICT services. Services that are exported might include cloud services, software services, start-ups, data stewardship, and artificial intelligence services. A firm in Estonia can be established entirely online in just a few hours and from almost anywhere in the world, thanks to technological solutions, including identity-card applications. Furthermore, Estonia is the also first country to offer e-residency to non-residents. Thus, the Estonian government provides the freedom and business environment to start and manage a company remotely. This is how it is relatively convenient to run a company, especially a service-related company, and this explains a large share of small-size service-exporting firms in Estonia (30% of service exports volume).[8] Until 2020, exports of Estonian services to Japan were driven by travel services (Japanese tourists coming to Estonia) and other business services, including trade-related services (Figure 3.7). Estonian imports from Japan have been driven by transport and travel services during 2010–2020. However, Estonian imports of ICT services have also increased in 2020, comprising already 16% of Estonian service imports from Japan (Figure 3.7).

Although ICT services exports to Japan comprise already 10%, the ICT services to Japan were only 0.6% of Estonian exports of ICT services in 2019, dropping to 0.3% in 2020 (Eurostat). As Japan's share in Estonian total service exports was

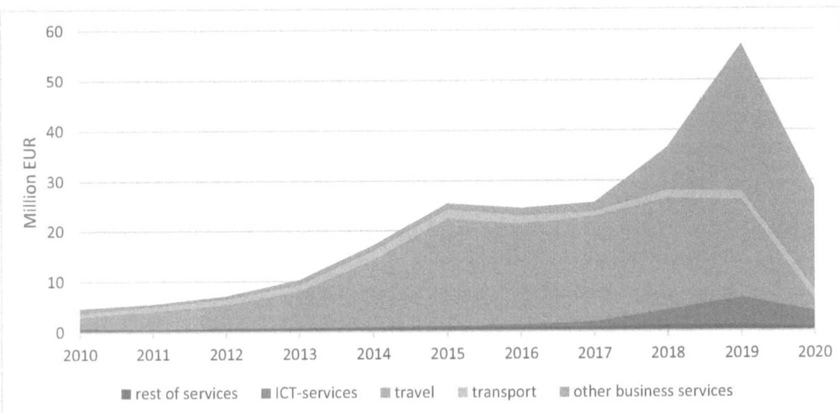

Figure 3.6 Estonian services exports to Japan, million euros, 2010–2020

Source: Eurostat data 2010–2020, accessed 11.10.2021, author's calculations.

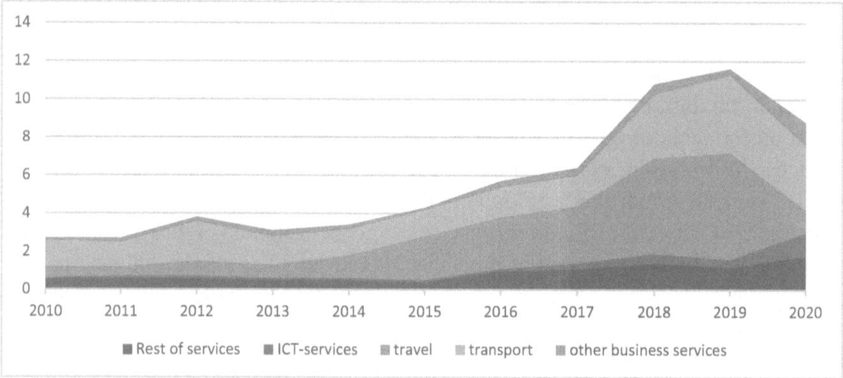

Figure 3.7 Estonian services imports from Japan, million euros, 2010–2020

Source: Eurostat data 2010–2020, accessed 11.10.2021, author's calculations.

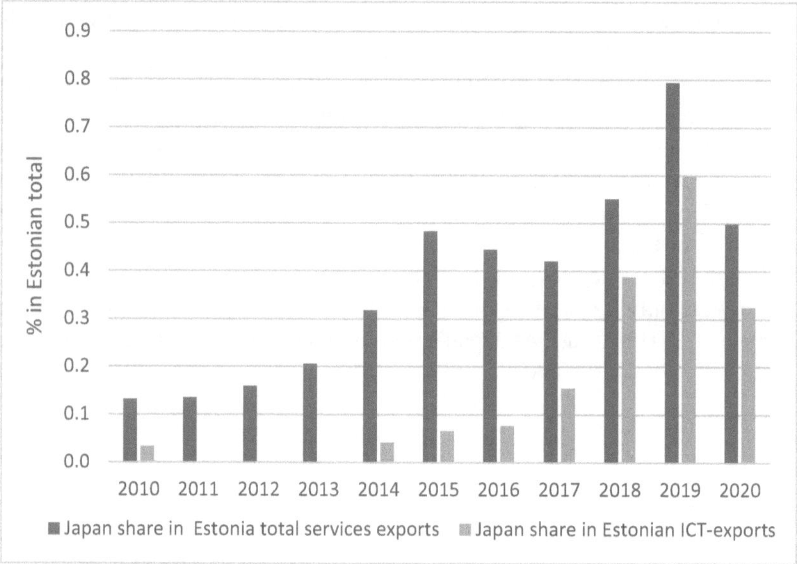

Figure 3.8 Share of Japan in Estonian total services exports and ICT services exports, million euros, 2010–2020

Source: Data retrieved from Eurostat. Accessed 11.10.2021, author's calculations.

0.5%, ICT services to Japan comprised 0.3% of Estonian ICT services exports in 2020. This shows that there is still potential to find a Japanese market for Estonian ICT services (Figure 3.8).

In conclusion, (1) cultural contacts are essential to enhance service trade and investments; (2) service trade and FDI should be analysed together, and that balance is calculated as the net of "exports of services *plus* investment inflows" and "imports of services *plus* investment outflows"; and (3) there is a high potential of ICT service exports from Estonia to Japan.

Service trade, FDI, and economic indicators' relationship

For analysing the factors that may constrain the service trade and FDI, Estonia and Japan are compared within the sample of 64 countries according to the following variables: (1) STRI, (2) Ease of doing business index, (3) Ease of doing trading index, (4) GDP per capita, (5) ratio of FDI inflow to GDP, (6) ratio of FDI outflow to GDP, (7) FDI inflow per capita, (8) FDI outflow per capita, (9) service exports per capita, (10) service imports per capita, (11) ratio of service export to service imports, and (12) FDI Restrictiveness Index.

STRI quantifies the service trade restrictions and is measured higher in Estonia than in Japan (39 vs. 27) (Table 3.3), However, it is easier to do business in Estonia than in Japan, as is described by the "ease of doing business" "index (81 vs. 78) (Table 3.3). Ease of doing trade index quantifies the standards of starting a business, getting credit, and paying taxes. Hence, Estonia ranks the highest with a maximum of 100 points, compared to 86 in Japan. The significant contrast is shown for FDI inflows, as Estonian inflows were 2300 USD per capita vs. 115 USD in Japan. Moreover, FDI is more restricted in Japan than in Estonia.

Table 3.3 FDI and service trade-related indicators, 2020 (or latest available data)

Indicator	*Mean (n = 64)*	*St. Deviation (n = 64)*	*Estonia*	*Japan*	*World*
Index: service trade restriction	42	8	39	27	
Index: Ease of Doing Business	74	8	81	78	
Index: Ease of Doing Business Trading	85	15	100	86	
GDP per capita current prices, USD	23080	21165	23740	40063	11339
FDI inflow % of GDP	3.4	4.2	9.8	0.3	1.8
FDI outflow % GDP	1.6	2.3	6.3	4.5	1.5
FDI Inflow per capita, current prices, USD	1030	2804	2297	115	201
FDI outflow per capita, current prices, USD	639	1321	1484	1787	182
Service exports per capita, USD	4031	8069	6064	1635	807
Service imports per capita, USD	3905	9684	4359	1626	771
Ratio of export of services to imports of services	1.2	0.5	1.4	1.0	1.0
FDI restrictiveness index	9.5	8.6	1.8	5.2	

Source: Data retrieved from Eurostat, UNCTAD, OECD, WTO, CIA. Accessed 05.08.2021, author's calculations.

For Estonia and Japan, large differences were registered for service exports per capita (6000 versus 1600 USD, respectively) and FDI inflows per capita (2300 versus 115 USD). This shows Estonia´s dependence on international markets. On the contrary, Japan scored higher than Estonia for outward flows (1900 versus 1500 USD), showing Japanese interest to invest abroad. The relationship between the indexes and the economic indicators were calculated using Pearson correlation coefficients (Table 3.4). A correlation coefficient is a value that ranges from +1 to −1, with 1 indicating that there is a perfect positive linear correlation between the two variables. Hence, as one variable increases, so does the other.

Table 3.4 Pearson correlation coefficients between indexes and economic indicators

	services_ trade_ restriction_ index	*Ease of Doing Business Trading*	*FDI Restriction Index*	*FDI_ Inflow_ per_ capita*	*FDI outflow_ per_ capita*	*Service exports per capita USD*	*Service imports per capita USD*
services_ trade_ restriction_ index	1.00	−0.186	**0.674****	−0.102	−0.201	−0.115	−.100
Ease of doing business trading	−0.186	1.00	**−0.449****	0.132	**0.280***	**0.257***	.188
FDI restriction index	**0.674****	**−0.449****	1.00	−0.155	−0.230	−0.241	−.190
FDI_ Inflow_ per_capita	−0.102	0.132	−0.155	1.00	**0.715****	**0.942****	**.925****
FDI outflow_ per_capita	−0.201	**0.280***	−0.230	**0.715****	1.00	**0.754****	**.687****
Service exports per capita USD	−0.115	**0.257***	−0.241	**0.942****	**0.754****	1.00	**.981****
Service imports per capita USD	−0.100	0.188	−0.190	**0.925****	**0.687****	**0.981****	1,00

Source: Data retrieved from Eurostat, UNCTAD, OECD, WTO, CIA. Accessed 05.08.2021,

Author’s calculations, * significant at 0.05 level (in bold), **significant at 0.01 level (in bold)

As assumed, ease of doing business trading is positively correlated with service exports per capita (r = 0.26) and FDI outflow (r = 0.28), both significant at 0.05 level.

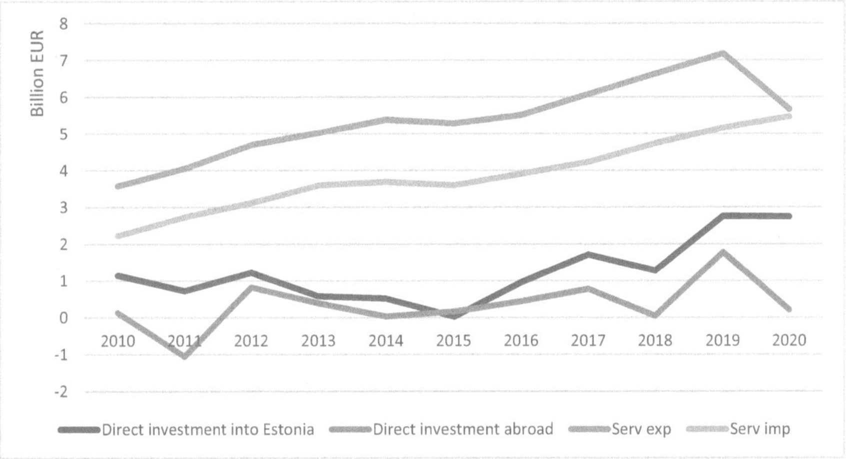

Figure 3.9 Estonian FDI and service trade, 2010–2020

Source: Data retrieved from Bank of Estonia; Statistics Estonia, accessed 05.08.2021.

Furthermore, negative correlation scores were reached for trade and FDI restriction indexes with all the FDI and service-related economic variables. However, strong and statistically significant positive correlations were marked between FDI and service trade per capita, with positive correlation coefficients from 0.75 to 0.94. This shows that if FDI flows increase, service exports would also increase, being the evidence to capture service and FDI flows together (Figure 3.9).

Trade barriers (ranging from domestic regulations, licensing, certification, etc.) are not easy to solve. For instance, in 2019, there was only one service barrier that the European Commission managed to solve, out of 40 barriers worldwide (Cernat, 2021).

Conclusion

Service trade is recognized as a growing form of economic activity; however, it is severely hit by the COVID-19 pandemic. With FDI, services may bring valuable benefits to countries, including the capital itself and the transfer of technological know-how and intellectual property rights, knowledge of export markets with improved export capacities, and opportunities. Selling or purchasing services and enterprises plays a crucial role in establishing competitive enterprises, creating jobs, and setting up cross-country supply chains. Furthermore, FDI is often accomplished as a result of the requirement by the countries to trade in FDI-related services, for example, accounting, software, or legal services. A strong correlation was identified between the FDI and service trade per capita. It was noticed that FDI and service-trade-related indicators were negatively influenced by the STRI and FDI-restrictiveness index, thus trade barriers impacting the trade and FDI flows negatively. For example, some service sectors in Japan may require board members to have Japanese nationality.

The data on service trade and FDI was derived from the Balance of Payments surveys that are in charge of national central banks, thus obtaining service trade with investment indicators and some indexes. The results showed that the exports of services and FDI inflows were conceptually similar and should be captured together, as stipulated also in GATS. However, in the current economic analysis, the FDI and service trade are two separate trading elements. Therefore, capturing FDI in conjunction with service trade is recommended and relevant balance to be calculated. As regards services, cross-border supply may become more prevailing in the next years, as businesses may take decisions to exit international markets, and, therefore, FDI flows may continue to decrease. Gravity model was theoretically used to explain why the flows between Estonia and Japan are assumed to be insignificant – Estonian economy is small, and the distance between two countries is large. In 2020, Estonian services exports to Japan have increased by six fold compared to 2010, peaking in 2019 with 57 million EUR. However, in 2020, services exports from Estonia to Japan declined by twofold compared to 2019, also due to the decrease in travel services, as tourism was hit the most in the COVID-19 crisis. On the other hand, FDI inflows to Estonia from Japan started to occur in 2016 with 10 million euros with the threefold increase by 2020, with some decline compared to 2019. For Estonia and Japan, the largest differences were registered for service exports per capita (6000 versus 1600 USD, respectively) and FDI inflows per capita (2300 versus 115 USD). This shows Estonia's dependence on international markets. On the contrary, Japan's outward flows per capita were larger than in Estonia (1900 vs 1500 USD), showing Japanese interest to invest abroad.

The cultural contacts are essential to enhance service trade and investments. In 2021, Estonia and Japan celebrated their centenary of friendship, acknowledging that cultural contacts were essential to enhance service trade and FDI volumes and establish a good partnership between the two distant countries by geography. Furthermore, as Estonia is famous worldwide as a small country with seven unicorns and knowledge-intensive sectors, a high potential exists regarding ICT-service exports from Estonia to Japan. Trade relations between Estonia and Japan could continue enhancing, if bilateral discussions could consider all the opportunities and acknowledge the possibilities to gain from service trade and foreign trade investment.

Notes

1 Based on UNCTAD dataset (https://unctadstat.unctad.org/wds/TableViewer/tableView.aspx).
2 https://unctadstat.unctad.org/wds/TableViewer/tableView.aspx?ReportId=96740
3 Trade Policy STRI regulatory database accessible through http://i-tip.wto.org/services/, basis for the STRI calculation; 2020 information available.
4 http://i-tip.wto.org/services/default.aspx. The Services Trade Restrictiveness Index database contains information on trade restrictions in the following sectors: computer

services, construction, professional services (legal, accounting, engineering, and architecture), telecommunication, distribution, audiovisual services, transport (air, maritime, road freight, and rail freight), courier, financial services (commercial banking, insurance), and logistics services (storage and warehouses).

5 www.cia.gov/the-world-factbook/field/ease-of-doing-business-index-scores

6 Based on Bank of Estonia data.

7 Japan was among the world's largest foreign direct investors together with the United States of America and the Netherlands in 2019 (UNCTAD, 2020).

8 Statistics Estonia service trade statistics database

4 Trade and FDI between Japan and Spain

Makiko Narita

Introduction

After Spain's inclusion into the European Union (EU) in 1986, foreign direct investment (FDI) increased and the country achieved high growth. However, in the 1990s, Central and Eastern European countries gained attention as being promising investment destinations. Low labour costs, involvement in the EU market, and skilled labour attracted many companies, including Japanese companies (Narita, 2000). In this context, the relocation of companies from Southern European countries to Central and Eastern European countries also occurred. Spain failed to effectively attract FDI in many industrial sectors (Turrión, 2005).

This chapter aims at analysing which industries are competitive and which attract FDI in a changing environment characterised by events like the global financial crisis of the 2000s and the conclusion of the economic partnership agreement (EPA) between Japan and the EU. To describe the characteristics of trade between Japan and Spain and Japanese direct investment to Spain, data from various sources were used: Trade and Investment Statistics by the Japan External Trade Organization (JETRO), Trade Statistics of Japan by the Ministry of Finance, and DataInvex by Spain's Ministry of Industry, Trade and Tourism. To examine the attractiveness of FDI, indicators provided by the World Economic Forum's (WEF) global competitiveness report were used.

This chapter compares the factors of FDI in Spain and Poland. Since the 1990s, unlike Spain, Poland has not experienced negative growth rates, even during the global financial crisis (Figure 4.1). Poland is one of the most attractive investment destinations for Japanese companies among Central and Eastern European countries. Between 2013 and 2018, Poland was the biggest beneficiary of Japanese FDI among the Visegrad Group members (Dzienis, 2021, p. 72). A comparison with Poland, which is smaller than Spain in terms of GDP and GDP per capita and has a similar market size (Table 4.1), will help us identify Spain's advantages and the industries in which it can be competitive.

DOI: 10.4324/9781003274933-4

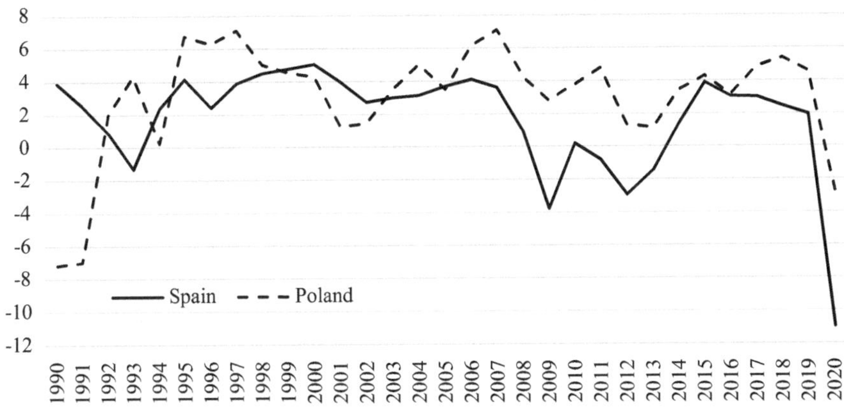

Figure 4.1 Growth rate (%)

Source: IMF, World Economic Outlook database.

Table 4.1 Spain and Poland

	Spain	*Poland*
Population (2020)	47.11 million	37.96 million
GDP (2020)	1278.21 billion USD	594.18 billion USD
GDP per capita (2020)	27132 USD	15654 USD
Growth rate (2020)	−10.96%	−2.72%
Unemployment rate (2020)	15.53%	3.16%
Export to Japan (2020)	3158 million USD	940 million USD
Export from Japan (2020)	2157 million USD	2854 million USD
Japanese firms (October 2020)	373 firms	356 firms

Source: IMF World Economic Outlook database, Ministry of Finance Trade Statistics of Japan, and Ministry of Foreign Affairs Annual Report of Statistics on Japanese Nationals Overseas.

Trade between Japan and Spain

Japan is one of the largest trading nations in the world, with exports of $640 billion and imports of $634.1 billion in 2020, according to trade statistics by JETRO. The EPA between Japan and the EU came into force in February 2019 and was expected to promote trade and investment between the two countries not only through the elimination or reduction of tariffs at a high level but also through the establishment of overarching rules for intellectual property. Even though Spanish–Japanese trade does not account for a significant proportion of either Japan's exports (around 0.4%) or Spain's exports (around 0.9%), the EPA is expected to further evolve the economic relationship between Japan and Spain. The reduction or elimination of tariffs under EPAs has led to an increase in trade between Japan and Spain (JETRO, 2020b). Japan's exports to Spain were dominated by machinery and transport equipment throughout the 2010s. According to the trade statistics from the Ministry of Finance, it accounted for 78.1% of Japan's exports to Spain in 2011 and 74.2% in 2020. In 2020, transport equipment accounted for 47.2%, general machinery accounted for 16.4%, and electrical equipment accounted for 10.5%. With regard to Japanese imports, and therefore Spanish exports, chemical products account for a large proportion. In 2011, it accounted for 44% of all imports, and, in 2020, it accounted for 22.3% of all imports. Among chemical products, imports of pharmaceuticals accounted for a significant share in the 2010s, 19.2% in 2011, and 10.7% in 2020. In 2020, meat accounted for 17.4% of the total import, and transport equipment accounted for 13.9%. The trade specification index (TSI) is an index for measuring international competitiveness. This is a measure of the competitiveness or comparative advantage of each trade item between two countries. It is calculated by dividing net exports (exports minus imports) by total trade, which is the sum of exports and imports, and takes a value between 1 and −1. For the purposes of this chapter, the Ministry of Finance's trade statistics is used to calculate the TSI from the value of Japan's exports and imports. A TSI close to 1 indicates that Japan has a comparative advantage, and a TSI close to −1 indicates that Spain has a comparative advantage.

The TSIs for the main products of trade between Japan and Spain are summarised in Figure 4.2. The sectors in which Japan has a comparative advantage over Spain are general machinery, electrical appliances, transport equipment, and precision machinery. In particular, the values for machinery and transport

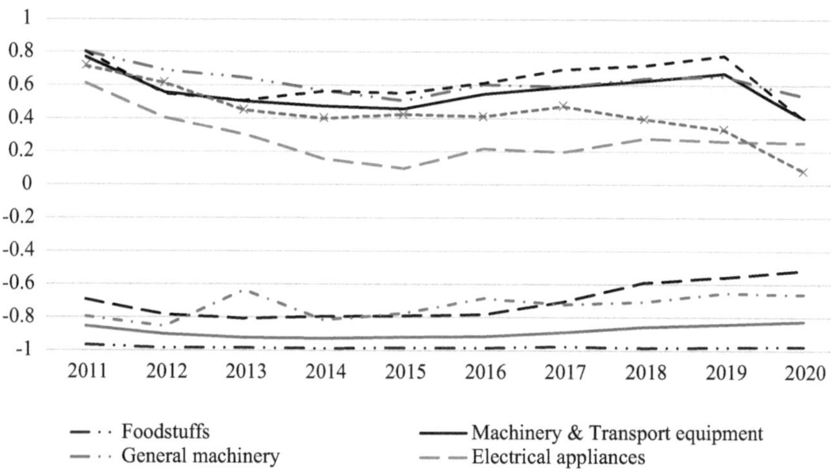

Figure 4.2 Trade specification index

Source: Own elaboration based on Ministry of Finance, Trade Statistics of Japan.

equipment remained high in the 2010s. Figure 4.2 also shows that, for general machinery and precision machinery, the TSI in Japan shows a downward trend.[1] Nevertheless, it can be argued that Japan still has a comparative advantage in manufacturing, which requires relatively advanced technology. On the other hand, the industries where Spain has a comparative advantage are foodstuffs, clothing, and chemical products (pharmaceuticals). Foodstuffs and clothing are not highly technological industries but pharmaceuticals are, and, therefore, Spain has a comparative advantage in this area and can be judged to be competitive.

Japanese foreign investment in Spain

Japan is an important investor in Spain, although it does not account for a large proportion of direct investment from Japan. The number of Japanese greenfield projects in Spain during 2016–2020 was 109, the eighth highest in the world. Japanese direct investment in Spain amounted to €729 million in 2020, accounting for 3.1% of direct investment in Spain (ICEX, 2021).

According to Figure 4.3 which shows gross direct investment in Spain, Japanese direct investment in Spain was considerable in the 2010s. In 2018, direct investment from Japan was huge, at approximately €4 billion.

In the industrial sector, Table 4.2 shows that much of Japan's investments were made in the manufacturing and service industries. The manufacturing industry

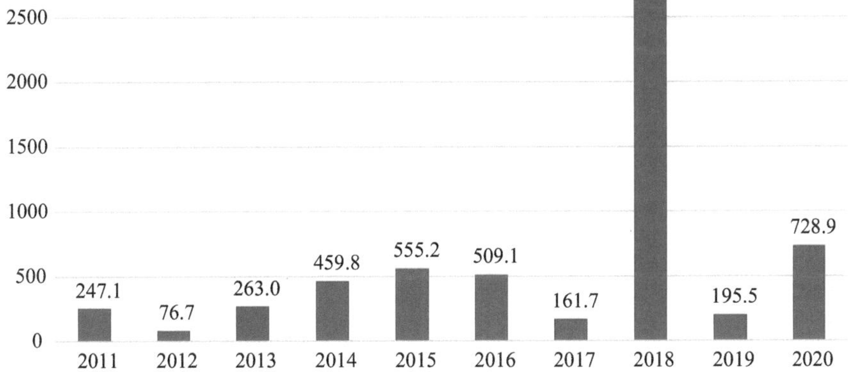

Figure 4.3 Japanese direct investment in Spain (gross, millions of euros)

Source: Own elaboration based on Ministerio de Indusria, Comercio y Turismo.

Table 4.2 Japanese direct investment in Spain by the industrial sector (% of total)

	2011	*2012*	*2013*	*2014*	*2015*	*2016*	*2017*	*2018*	*2019*	*2020*
Extraction of crude oil and natural gas				10.5						
Beverage production	27.6									
Paper industry							7.6			
Chemical industry	17.7	14.0		7.9				76.0		
Manufacture of pharmaceutical products									30.9	
Manufacture of metal products, except machinery			45.2			81.7				
Manufacture of computer and electronic products	17.0									
Manufacture of machinery and equipment		18.8	18.6							
Manufacture of motor vehicles and trailers		5.7			27.2		39.7		6.4	
Electricity, gas, steam, and air supply	31.5	22.1			18.9					
Water collection, purification, and distribution			33.1	7.8						
Sale and repair of motor vehicles and motorcycles										23.8
Wholesale and retail trade, excluding motor vehicles		5.6			50.8		37.0	20.7	8.8	46.8
Storage and ancillary transport activity				8.0						
Activities of film, video, and TV programmes		27.9								
Programming, consultancy, and other related activities				60.9		9.1			42.1	24.9
Sports, recreational, and entertainment activities							6.2			

Source: Own elaboration based on Ministerio de Industria, Comercioy Turismo, Datalnvex.

Note: Only industries that received more than 5% of total investment are extracted.

saw high percentages of direct investment in metal products, machinery, and pharmaceuticals, as well as motor vehicles. In the service sector, investment in wholesale and retail trade and programming and consultancy activities accounted for a high proportion of Japan's direct investment. Investment in the chemical industry and infrastructure-related industries, such as gas, was also significant. Japanese firms located in Spain are more likely to be in the service sector than those in Central and Eastern European countries. As of October 2020, there were 373 Japanese companies located in Spain, of which 98 are in the manufacturing sector, 70 in the accommodation and food services sector, and 50 are in the wholesale and retail trade (Ministry of Foreign Affairs, 2020).[2]. Of the 356 Japanese companies operating in Poland, 113 are in the manufacturing sector and 102 in the wholesale and retail trade sectors. On the other hand, in Central and Eastern Europe, the presence of manufacturing companies, especially in the automobile and automobile parts industries, is more noticeable.[3].

The same characteristics can be observed in the investment projects of Japanese firms in the 2010s. Although there are investment projects in the automobile industry, such as Takahata and Ube Industries,[4] a number of investment projects were carried out in the services sector, including Fast Retailing's expansion into Spain in 2017 and Hitachi Transport System's establishment of a local subsidiary in 2019. Japanese investment in Poland in the 2010s was dominated by automotive and auto parts companies such as Toyota, Bridgestone, Mabuchi Motor, and Nippon Seiki.[5] In the late 2010s, Spain attracted Japanese investment in knowledge-intensive industries, such as pharmaceuticals and IT. In the pharmaceutical sector, AGC acquired a pharmaceutical company in 2019, and Takeda bought a pharmaceutical venture in 2019. IT-related investment deals include Rakuten's investment in Globo in 2018 and Nippon Telegraph and Telephone Corporation (NTT) Data's establishment of an AI consolidation centre and NTT.Com's acquisition of CAPSiDE in 2019.

Attractiveness for FDI in Spain: a comparison with Poland

The Financial Times publishes "FDI European Cities and Regions of the Future" which ranks the best and brightest European cities and regions for investment in five categories: economic potential, human capital and lifestyle, cost effectiveness, connectivity, and business friendliness. In the latest 2020 edition, the Spanish regions with the highest overall ratings are Catalonia (15th) and Madrid (18th).[6] Madrid is rated high for human capital, while Catalonia is rated high for connectivity and economic potential. In the Polish regions, Silesia ranked high in cost effectiveness and Masovian Voivodeship in terms of cost effectiveness and business friendliness. Regarding the factors for attracting FDI, Dunning (1977) points out the location-specific advantages that a firm can acquire by expanding into a foreign country. This chapter examines location-specific advantages to better understand the factors that can influence a firm's decision on where to locate when it expands its activities to a foreign country. Factors that have been identified to be responsible for attracting FDI to Spain include relatively low labour costs in Europe, a high-quality workforce, access to the European market, and well-developed infrastructure.[7] Narita (2016) points out that Spain still gained the advantages of having relatively lower wages and higher education standards compared to what other European countries offered in the 2010s. The Investment Office plays an important role in direct investment from Japan to Spain (Narita, 2021). Financial Times (2020) ranked Catalonia as being the fourth and Madrid as being the sixth in the category of FDI strategy, which evaluates strategies for promoting FDI. In terms of access to the large European markets, the distance between the capitals of the two countries and the main European market is 1550 km (Madrid), which is further than Warsaw (832 km).[8]. Spain is at a disadvantage because of the greater cost of transporting its products. For other factors, the indicators in the WEF's Global Competitiveness report were used. Table 4.3 compares the factors associated with FDI location advantage.

Table 4.3 Indicators of competitiveness

	Spain	*Poland*
Labour market (0–100) (2)	61.1	59.9
Labour costs (euros per hour in 2020) (3)	22.8	11.0
Redundancy costs (week of salary)	17.3	18.8
Flexibility of wage determination	5.1	5.5
Active labour market policies	3.9	3.6
Reliance on professional management	4.7	4.1
Pay and productivity	3.7	4.2
Skill (0–100) (2)	71.6	72.1
Mean years of schooling (years)	9.8	12.3
Quality of vocational training	4.5	3.5
Digital skills among active populations	4.3	4.3
Ease of finding skilled employees	4.6	4.1
School life expectancy (years)	17.9	16.4
Infrastructure (0–100) (2)	90.3	81.2
Quality of road infrastructure	5.7	4.3
Efficiency of train services	5.4	3.9
Efficiency of air transport services	5.6	4.8
Efficiency of seaport services	5.4	4.5
Electricity supply quality (% of output)	9.5	5.6
Business dynamism (0–100) (2)	67.3	62.0
Cost of starting a business (% of GNI per capita)	4.0	11.8
Time to start a business (days)	12.5	37.0
Attitudes towards entrepreneurial risk	3.8	3.9
Growth of innovative companies	4.0	3.9
Institutions (0–100) (2)	65.1	56.4
Efficiency of legal framework in challenging regulations	3.4	2.5
Incidence of corruption (0–100)	58.0	60.0
Intellectual property protection	4.8	4.1
Government ensuring policy stability	4.2	2.9
Innovation capability (0–100) (2)	64.3	49.7
Patent application (per million population)	28.92	12.68
R&D expenditures (% of GDP)	1.2	1.0
Trademark applications (per million population)	7361.95	3190.7

Source: Own elaboration based on WEF (2019) and Eurostat database.

Note: (1) Values range from 1 to 7 scale, where 7 represents best.
(2) Scores are on a 0 to 100 scale, where 100 represents the optimal situation or "frontier".
(3) Labour costs are not included in the indicators of WEF ranking.

Labour costs in 2020 are much lower in Poland (€11.0) than in Spain (€22.8). Therefore, Spain has no advantage in terms of labour costs. The score for the labour market is slightly higher in Spain than in Poland. However, it is often pointed out that there are problems in the Spanish labour market and that the labour market is not sufficiently advantageous for firms. In interviews with Japanese firms operating in Spain, the rigidity of the labour market was pointed out to be one of the operational difficulties (Narita, 2021). In terms of the quality of labour, the score is slightly higher in Poland than in Spain, indicating a better quality of labour in Poland. The mean year of schooling is longer in Poland, but the quality of vocational training is higher in Spain, where it is easier to find skilled employees. With regard to digital skills, the conditions are almost the same in this field. As for infrastructure, Spain is better developed and has an advantage. Both the efficiency of transport and the quality of electricity supply have higher scores, indicating that the country has the necessary infrastructure for production. Regarding the indicators of business dynamism, the cost and time to start a business are lower in Spain, which makes it easier to start a business. However, Spain has a lower value as an indicator of attitudes towards entrepreneurial risk. For institutions, the score for the indicator listed in Table 4.3 is 65.1 for Spain and 56.4 for Poland, and each indicator has a higher value for Spain. The value of each indicator was also higher in Spain than in Poland. Therefore, Poland needs to improve in this respect to become a more attractive destination for FDI. Last, Spain scores higher than Poland in terms of innovation capability, reflecting the difference between patent applications and trademark applications.

Conclusion

This chapter attempts to identify which Spanish industries are competitive in the 2010s, both in terms of trade and FDI. From trade with Japan, Spain does not have a comparative advantage over Japan in manufacturing industries that require a high level of technology, such as machinery, transport equipment, and precision instruments. However, Spain does have a competitive edge in chemical products, such as pharmaceuticals. In terms of investment projects in Poland, there were a relatively large number of projects related to cars and motor vehicles. In Spain, although there were some automotive projects, the most prominent investments were in the manufacturing sector (chemicals and pharmaceuticals) and in the service sector (IT, wholesale and retail trade, and infrastructure). In the late 2010s, Spain attracted Japanese investment projects in knowledge-intensive industries such as pharmaceuticals and IT. Spain is at a disadvantage compared to Poland in terms of access to the main European markets and labour costs. Meanwhile, Spain is highly rated on the indicators of infrastructure, business dynamism, innovation capacity, and institutions. Therefore, while it may be necessary to focus on the automotive industry, which has been the mainstay of Spain's development, it is also necessary to take measures to make Spain more competitive in knowledge-intensive industries such as IT services and pharmaceuticals, which have attracted the attention of Japanese companies, as well as in infrastructure projects. Hence, Spain should focus its resources on actionable measures to improve its competitiveness in these knowledge-intensive industries. The COVID-19 pandemic will have a significant impact on upcoming direct investment. Many Japanese companies are concerned about the contraction of economic activity due to the spread of COVID-19 (JETRO, 2020a). While it is unclear when the pandemic will fully pass and economic activity will resume, there is a great possibility of accelerated corporate restructuring and withdrawal (e.g. Nissan plans to close its Barcelona plant at the end of 2021).

Notes

1 In terms of semiconductor- manufacturing equipment, Japan has a comparative advantage as it has maintained a high TSI value.
2 This includes companies established locally by Japanese nationals.
3 Many Japanese companies operating in Central and Eastern European countries are in the manufacturing sector. For example, of the 276 companies operating in the Czech Republic, 108 are in the manufacturing sector.
4 Takahata opened a plant for mechanical parts for cars in 2019, while Ube Industries acquired a majority stake in compounder Repsol in 2019.
5 Toyota invested in an additional plant in Poland in 2016; Bridgestone invested to increase tyre production in 2017; Mabuchi Motor established a production base for motors for automotive electrical equipment in 2017; and Nippon Seiki established a company to manufacture in-car instruments and indicators in 2019
6 The regional rankings are divided into three size categories: large regions with a population of 4 million or more, mid-sized regions with a population between 1.5 million and 4 million, and small regions with a population of fewer than 1.5 million. The regions mentioned here, Madrid, Catalonia, Silesia, and Masovian Voivodeship, belong to "large region". In terms of cities, the most highly rated cities were Madrid (11th) and Barcelona (19th) in Spain and Warsaw (6th) and Stryków (17th) in Poland
7 These factors were also pointed out in interviews with Japanese companies operating in Spain. For details, see Narita (2021).
8 As Turrión (2005) shows, the distances are calculated as the average distance from Berlin and Paris weighted by the population of these cities. The distance from Barcelona, the capital of Catalonia, where many Japanese companies are located, is 1361 km.S

5 Deconstructing Indian outward foreign direct investment in UK

A case study analysis

Smita Shukla

Introduction

The UK has been a popular investment destination for foreign companies. Companies from worldwide markets have always exhibited interest in the UK. The inward FDI international investment position in the UK held by foreign companies has been on an average exhibited uptrend. Figure 5.1 represents the FDI (inward) position in the UK held by foreign companies since 2010.

At the same time, the inward FDI in the UK has exhibited mixed trends over last few years with substantial increase in the year 2016 due to some high-value

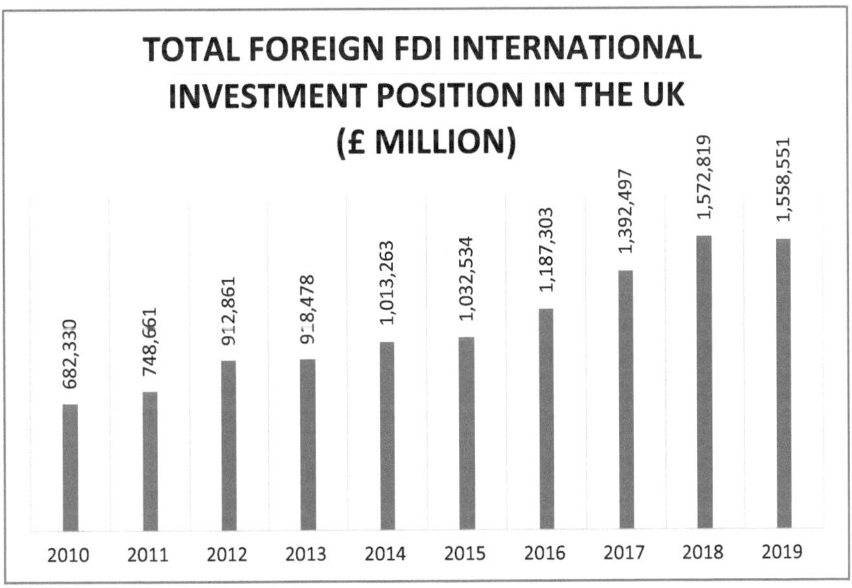

Figure 5.1 Inward FDI international investment position in the UK held by foreign companies in 2010–2019

Data Source: Office for National Statistics, UK [Foreign Direct Investment involving UK Companies. Retrieved September 2, 2021, from www.ons.gov.uk/businessindustryandtrade/business/businessinnovation/datasets/foreigndirectinvestmentinvolvingukcompanies2013inwardtables]

DOI: 10.4324/9781003274933-5

mergers and acquisitions by the foreign companies. The inward FDI as percentage of GDP in the UK in 2019 was 2%, and the average inward FDI over ten-year period starting from the year 2010 has been 3%.

The year-wise details of inward FDI flows in the UK are represented in Figure 5.2.

The UK and India have a shared business and political history. India also has had significant ties with the UK on account of being part of Commonwealth Nations block. Resurgent India, post liberalization, also generated the interest of British companies. Large and growing middle-class with rising consumer aspirations along with flourishing Indian economy offered an attractive potential for growth for the companies from the UK investing in India. Hence, despite the global uncertainty due to the current pandemic, the UK has continued to be sixth largest investing country in India over last few years including its investment in the financial year 2020–21. According to the data shared by National Investment Promotion and Facilitation Agency (India), there are over 572 British companies with a turnover of INR 3390 billion, directly employing over four lakh people in India.

Since the first decade of 2000, Indian companies have been prominent investors in the UK. An upward trend is witnessed in inward as well as outward FDI stock by the UK and Indian companies over last few years. The FDI stock is the accumulated value of all the previous investments calculated on net basis (value of investment minus the disinvestment). The stock of foreign direct investment between the UK and India since 2010 is represented in Figure 5.3.

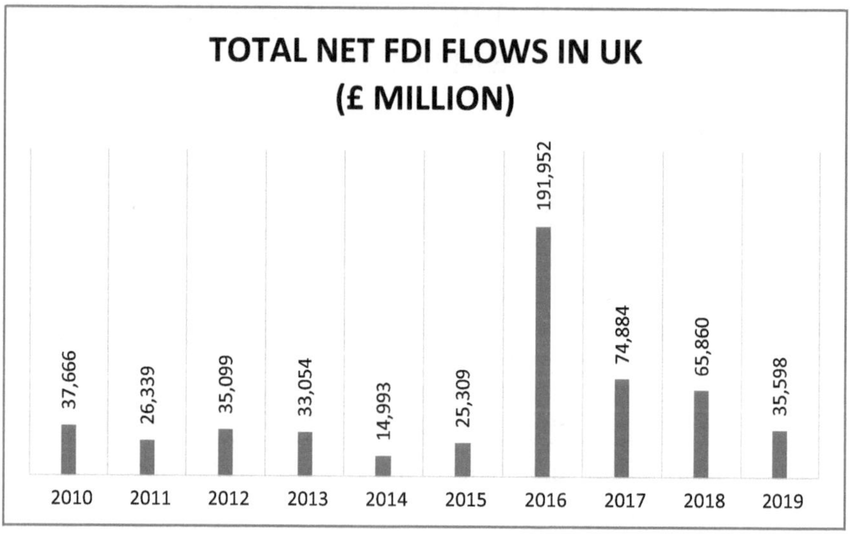

Figure 5.2 FDI flows into the UK by foreign companies (inward), 2010–2019

Data Source: Office for National Statistics, UK. Retrieved September 2, 2021, from www.ons.gov.uk/businessindustryandtrade/business/businessinnovation/datasets/foreigndirectinvestmentinvolvingukcompanies2013inwardtables]

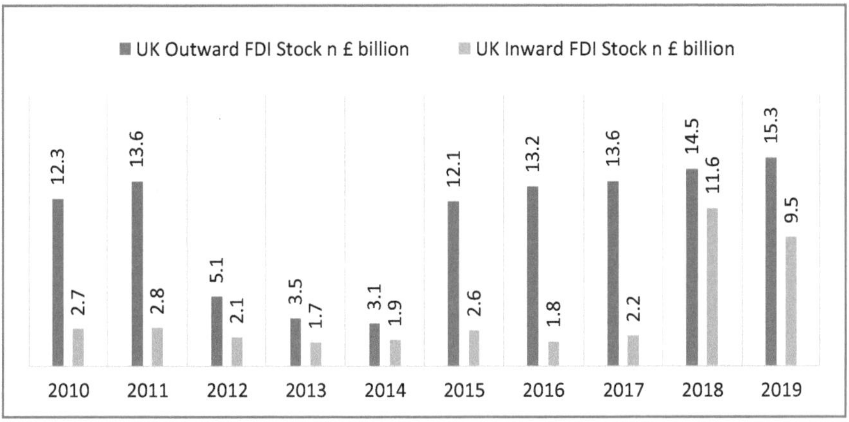

Figure 5.3 Stock of FDI between the UK and India, 2010–19

DataSource: Department of International Trade – Trade and Investment Factsheet 2021. Retrieved September 21, 2021, from www.gov.uk/government/statistics/trade-and-investment-factsheets-partner-names-beginning-with-g-to-i

In Figure 5.3, the UK outward FDI stock provides the total value of FDI by the UK investors in India, and the UK inward FDI stock provides the total value of FDI by Indian investors in the UK.

India has been the second top source market for FDI projects in UK in the years 2019–20 and 2020–21. Though the number of projects and jobs created by Indian companies in the UK reflected some downward trend in the year 2020–21 in comparison to the year 2019–20 (that had witnessed 120 project investments and creation of 5,429 jobs), the overall status of India being second top source market for FDI projects in the UK was maintained. According to the Department of International Trade (UK), the inward investment results from 2020 to 2021 exhibit that the United States was the top source market for FDI projects in the UK followed by India. The details of top 15 source countries for FDI projects in the UK in the year 2020–21 are as given in Table 5.1.

Within the UK, there are several regions that are attractive for Indian companies. For example, London has received maximum investment and has been popular as it is a global financial centre and a cosmopolitan city. It is also known for its vibrant start-up ecosystem. In addition to London, other major investment regions in the UK for Indian companies have been South Britain, North Britain and Midlands in the order of importance during five-year period starting from 2016–17 to 2020–21.

As per Grant Thornton-CII Britain Meets India reports for the period 2016–17 to 2020–21, the preferred regional investment destinations in Britain for the Indian companies are reflected in Figure 5.4.

Table 5.1 Top source markets for FDI projects in the UK (year 2020–21)

Country	*FDI Projects*	*New Jobs*
The United States	389	19,301
India	99	4,830
Germany	93	6,405
France	88	5,278
The Netherlands	72	2,674
Italy	66	1,215
Canada	58	1,052
Japan	51	1,463
Sweden	49	1,024
China	46	1,209
Ireland	42	1,097
Spain	41	714
Australia	40	659
Israel	33	677
Switzerland	29	515

Source: Department for International Trade inward investment results, 2020 to 2021. Retrieved September 24, 2021, from www.gov.uk/government/statistics/department-for-international-trade-inward-investment-results-2020-to-2021/department-for-international-trade-inward-investment-results-2020-to-2021-online-version

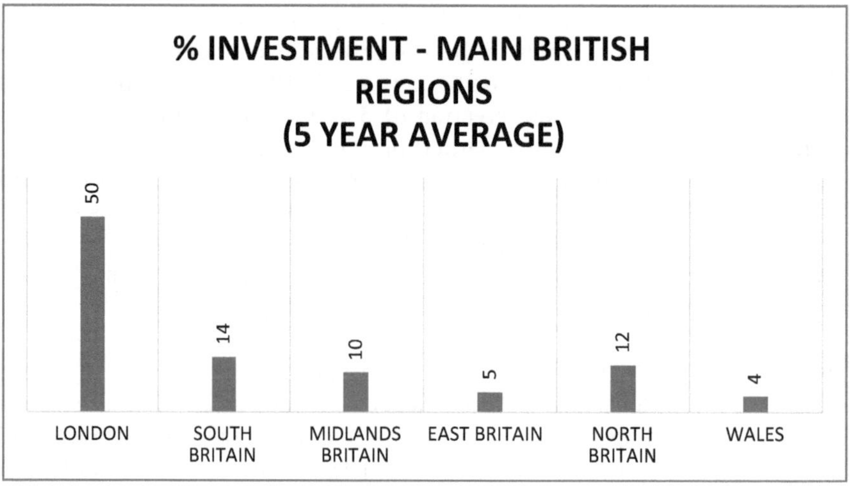

Figure 5.4 Investment destinations in Britain for Indian companies

Source: Britain Meets India Reports (2017 to 2021), Grant Thornton-CII. Retrieved September 3 from www.grantthornton.in/en/insights/and www.cii.in/publications.aspx

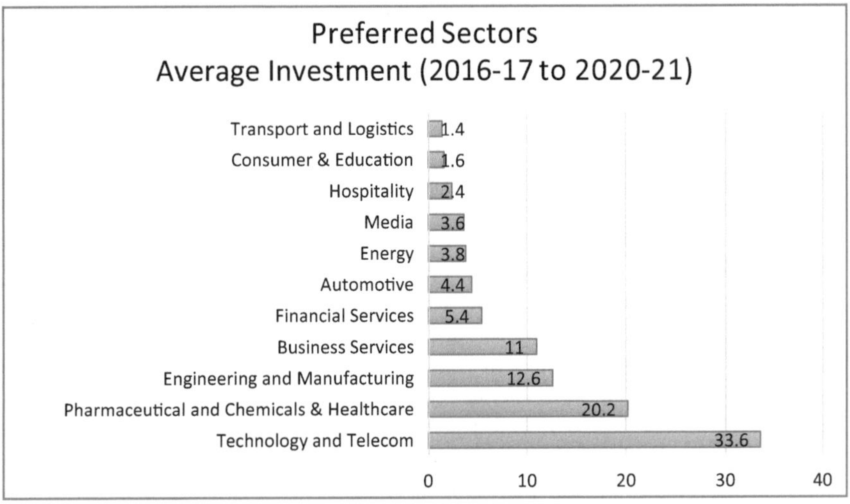

Figure 5.5 Preferred sectors for investment by Indian companies in Britain

Source: Britain Meets India Report 2021 – Grant Thornton-CII. Retrieved September 3, from www.grantthornton.in/en/insights/articles/india-meets-britain-tracker-2021/

The Grant-Thornton-CII 'Britain meets India' Reports from 2016–17 to 2020–21 also highlight the preferred sectors for investment by Indian companies in Britain based on an average of five-year period sectoral investment by the Indian companies in the UK starting from the year 2016–17 to 2020–21.

The most preferred sector for investment by the Indian companies in the UK has been Technology and Telecom sector followed by Pharmaceuticals, Chemicals and Healthcare sector and subsequently by the Engineering and Manufacturing sector and others. As per the Grant Thornton-CII 2021 report, there are 850 Indian companies in Britain operating with revenue worth 50.8 billion pounds and over 116,046 employees. Figure 5.5 represents preferred sectors of investment by Indian companies in the UK as based on an average of five-year period sectoral investment by Indian companies in the UK.

Key drivers for investment by Indian companies in Britain

The key drivers for investment by Indian companies in the UK are many. First and foremost, it has been that the UK has always been a springboard to Europe for the Indian companies. Familiar language, previous business and cultural ties including family ties of family-managed Indian businesses have also favoured the UK as an initial investment destination and as a gateway to Europe.

Indian companies that have had global ambitions have found it easy to start their business operations in Britain before moving to other European nations. Several

Indian pharmaceuticals, chemical and healthcare companies have invested in the UK for this reason. Sometimes access to distribution channels for products manufactured in India also has been a reason for investing in The UK. Some such examples are Secure Meters, TVS group companies, and some pharmaceutical companies like Wockhardt (the UK).

Britain also has been home to several world-class iconic brands, and this has also accentuated the interest of Indian companies in the UK. Several acquisitions by Tata group, TVS group, Mahindra and Mahindra group, Dhoot group indicate the same. Acquisition of brands like Jaguar and Land Rover, Corus, Norton, Hamleys, Tetley Tea and Optare are some cases to point. The acquisition of international iconic brands provides international market opportunities to the Indian companies.

The purpose of acquisition by the Indian companies also has been to get access to cutting-edge engineering practices, technical know-how, intellectual property rights, and research and development capabilities. The acquisitions made by Indian companies in the Engineering and Manufacturing, Technology and Telecom sector in the UK have been driven by engineering and design capabilities of UK companies and by the mutually beneficial relationships in this space.

Britain also has emerged as a technology hub with people and as well as technology capabilities. There also has been an agreement between TechUK and NASSCOM thereby launching UK–India tech alliance for collaboration in skills and innovation. The digital economy in the UK has also boosted investment in Technology and Telcom sector. UK's expertise in emerging technology spaces like AI, Blockchain and Internet of Things has also boosted technology investment in UK by Indian companies.

Opportunities in green energy and the application of technology in energy usage, monitoring, saving and technology-enabled energy solutions have also been attractive areas of investment by Indian companies.

The UK also has favourable tax regime and transparent legal system. The UK government offers tax credit for research and development activities conducted in the UK. Investments in the UK by Indian companies also have been driven by the fact that British government has announced that India is one of its foremost target countries for setting Free Trade Agreement. Several bilateral negotiations at top government level and interest exhibited by top political executives in both the countries have further encouraged Indian investments in the UK.

Despite Brexit and the COVID pandemic, Indian companies have continued their investments in the UK, and, as per Grant Thornton-CII reports (various years), the Indian companies have invested more in Britain in comparison to their combined investments in the EU.

In addition to overall key drivers for Indian investment in the UK, the identified sectoral drivers for investment by Indian companies in in the top preferred sectors in the UK are as given in Table 5.2.

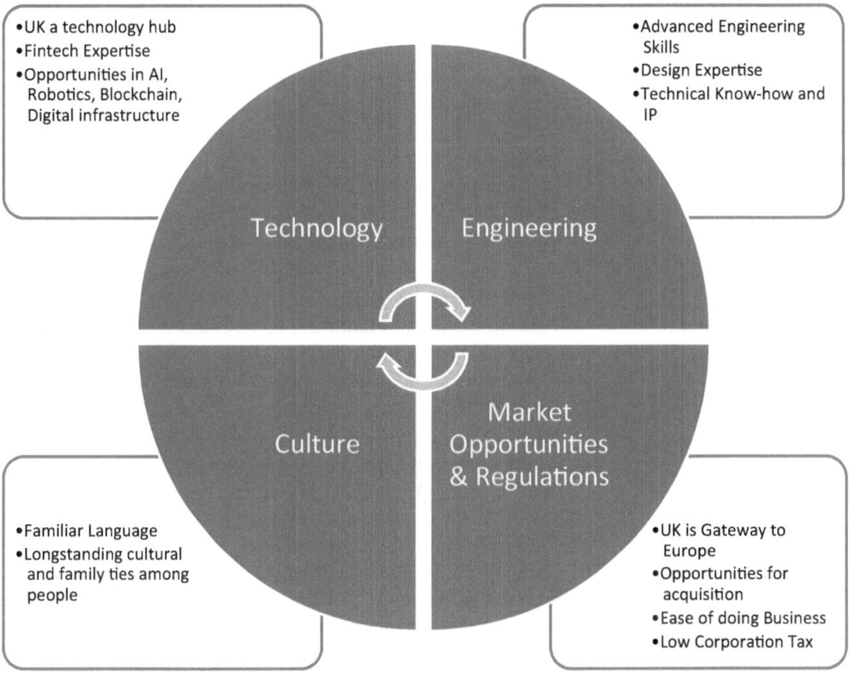

Figure 5.6 Key drivers for investment in the UK by Indian companies

Source: Factsheets of Department of International Trade (UK), 'India Meets Britain' tracker reports of Grant Thornton-CII (various years) and other industry and media reports.

Table 5.2 Sectoral drivers for investment by Indian companies in the UK

Sector	*Drivers*
Technology and Telecom	1. Technical know-how 2. Pool of talented human resource 3. Market opportunities in the sector because of UK's digital economy and digital infrastructure 4. Expertise in emerging technology areas like Blockchain, AI, IoT 5. Technology alliances between government bodies and as well as technology trade associations of the two nations (TechUK and NAASCOM) for collaboration and innovation 6. Innovation ecosystem 7. The UK still being springboard to Europe 8. Conducive tax and regulatory environment and ease in setting and doing business specifically for the start-ups

(Continued)

Table 5.2 (Continued)

Sector	*Drivers*
Pharmaceuticals, Chemicals and Healthcare	1. Entry to other European markets 2. Market opportunities within the UK in health care 3. Access to distribution channel for marketing products manufactured in India 4. Research and development capabilities 5. Conducive tax and regulatory environment and ease in setting and doing business
Engineering and Manufacturing including Automotive	1. Design and engineering skills and expertise 2. Research and development capabilities 3. Cutting-edge manufacturing technologies 4. Technology-enabled manufacturing 5. Conducive tax and regulatory environment and ease in setting and doing business
Financial Services and Business Services	1. London being international financial sector 2. Digital economy and digital infrastructure 3. Successful and innovative FinTech companies 4. UK being world-class educational hub 5. Opportunities in consulting, legal, research, insurance, medical and wellness and waste management services 6. Indian companies with vibrant operations in UK as potential customers 7. Ease of setting financial services firm in UK 8. Expertise in emerging technology areas like Blockchain, AI, IoT 9. Conducive regulatory environment and recent positive changes in regulations by governments including the central banks in two countries

Source: Factsheets of Department of International trade (UK), 'India Meets Britain' tracker reports of Grant Thornton-CII (various years) and other industry and media reports.

Indian investment in Britain – Secure Meters, Accord Healthcare, HCL, Tata Motors

Four case studies of Indian companies that have invested in the UK with different investment perspectives have been shortlisted to get insight into the interest and reasons for direct investments by Indian companies in the said sector in the UK. The case studies also offer insight on impact of Brexit and COVID-19 on the operations of the Indian companies. The shortlisted companies are:

- **Secure Meters (UK)** – Secure Meters is an energy-saving device company that is producing both the consumer and industrial technology-enabled energy saving and metering solutions for global markets and the UK. The company has been one of the fastest growing Indian companies in the UK over last several years before pandemic impacted the markets.

- **Accord Healthcare** – Accord Healthcare is a pharmaceuticals and chemical sector company that again holds the distinction of being one of the fastest growing Indian companies in the UK.
- **HCL Technologies UK** – HCL, a technology sector company, has held business interest in the UK since 1990s. It also has been one of the fastest growing technology companies in the UK and has been recognized for being an employer with best practices and has created local jobs for managing its operations in the UK.
- **Jaguar Land Rover Automotive Plc** – Jaguar Land Rover is an automotive engineering company that was formed after the acquisition of the iconic Jaguar and Land Rover brands by Tata Motors. Jaguar Land Rover operations have created more than 40,000 local jobs in the UK thereby making Tata Motors the largest Indian employer in the UK.

Case Study 1: Secure Meters (UK) Ltd

Secure Meters is a privately held Indian-origin company. It started its business operations as the first company in India manufacturing electronic electricity meters in the year 1987 in the state of Rajasthan. Since then, it has developed expertise in entire energy management stream focusing on using energy responsibly. Its solutions include smart grid metering and intelligent heating control systems with a presence in several countries worldwide and specifically in the UK.

The international presence of the company has been accentuated through organic as well as inorganic growth. The first acquisition of Secure Meters was Cewe Instruments in Sweden in the year 2006 followed by Horstmann Controls and AEMS acquisitions in the UK. The company has preferred to retain the acquired product brands in the UK and Sweden because of their recall value in the European region and Middle East. While the younger product brands such as Advanced Energy Monitoring Systems (AEMS) Limited that marketed Yatemeter have been merged within Secure.

The Cewe Instrument AB, with over 50 years of business history and presence in more than 50 countries in regions like South-East Asia, Middle-East and Europe, offers a range of smart instruments and solutions for electrical and energy measurement that are communication enabled and do data collection and processing for making the customers aware of their energy consumption and the carbon dioxide emission in electrical consumption.

Horstmann Controls is a leading manufacturer of controls for domestic heating systems and offers a range of smart solutions. The entity is also known for accuracy, quality and reliability of the products and has presence in many countries across Europe, Middle-East and Australia.

The Secure Meters focuses on high-precision manufacturing and on-time delivery. The company also has been a front runner in innovation in energy-saving solutions. In fact, it was the first company in India to produce electronic electricity meters, followed by first tamper-resistant electronic meters and later smart-energy-saving devices including the 'Liberty Prepayment System' that is pay as

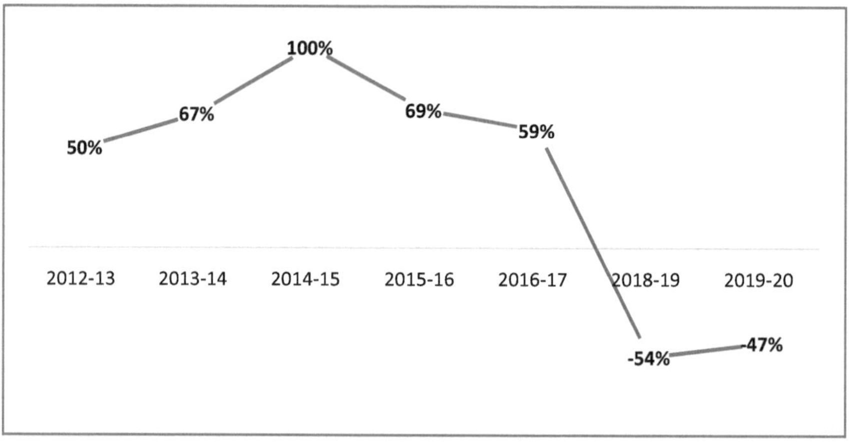

Figure 5.7 Turnover growth – Secure Meters (the UK), 2012–2020

Source: https://uk.globaldatabase.com/company/secure-meters-uk-limited. Retrieved on September 28, 2021.

you use system (introduced in Ireland in 1999) and 'Prodigy' in South-East Asia. The product 'Prodigy' helps electricity distribution companies in improving the monitoring and management of distribution transformers. The company's 'Bean-bag Care' product in the UK offers smart energy solution products for older adults (aged) that capture changes in daily routine and habits of the service users to indicate any deterioration in their health and ability and manage the temperature and humidity in home environment matching the routine of service user including the emergency alarm systems thereby helping the aged to live safely at home. The Secure Meters has received several awards for research and development in the energy sector.

As per Grant Thornton-CII India Meets Britain tracker reports, Secure Meters (UK) has the distinction of being one of very few Indian investing companies in the UK that performed exceedingly well in UK for six consecutive years (2013–14 to 2017–18) on the parameter of turnover performance. The company started facing turnover downturn from the year 2018–19 onwards and is currently in the recovery phase. The turnover of Secure Meters (UK) in a seven-year period starting from 2012–13 to 2019–20 has been as reflected in Figure 5.7.

Reasons for investment by Secure Meters in the UK

The company was keen on building global presence and with that intent it made its first acquisition of Cewe Instruments in Sweden in the year 2006. This acquisition was followed by another acquisition of Horstmann Controls and AEMS in the UK. The company has preferred to retain the acquired product brands in the UK and Sweden because of their recall value in the UK, European region and Middle East and was able to get inroads into multiple global markets.

The company, through the acquisitions, was also able to procure technical know-how and manufacturing expertise to make a strong foray in the technology-enabled home, office and industry energy solutions as well as technology-enabled energy monitoring, metering and saving products. The company also acquired strong research and development capabilities through its global acquisitions. The company, because of aforementioned acquisition advantages, has registered excellent financial performance over the years.

Impact of Brexit and COVID-19 on Secure Meters (UK) Ltd

One of the reasons for the downturn in the performance of the company since 2018–19 has been Brexit. The company has suffered some setback in performance owing to confusion and downturn in sales in European region due to Brexit. COVID-19-induced slowdown due to disruptions in sales and production operations also has negatively impacted the performance of the company. The company has also faced performance loss as it was slow in responding to transition in the UK from SMETS-1 meters that do not allow consumer to change the energy supplier to the SMETS-2 meters that allow consumer to change seamlessly between energy suppliers. The UK government had floated a program in 2018 to move from SMETS-1 to SMETS-2 meters for benefiting the consumers. The company is currently recovering from losses and holds a strong recovery and growth potential because of its technology-enabled energy saving and metering solutions and product portfolio.

Case Study 2: Accord Healthcare (the UK)

Accord Healthcare is an Indian-origin pharmaceutical company involved in the development, manufacturing and distribution of generic pharmaceutical products in more than 70 countries with majority in EMENA market (Europe, Middle-East and North-Africa) and with a recent foray in ASEAN market. The company has grown both organically as well as inorganically.

The company has developed extensive sales and marketing distribution network in Europe and Middle-East while basing itself in the UK. In fact, Accord Healthcare has been one of the fastest-growing pharmaceutical companies in the UK and Ireland. The company has two UK-based manufacturing sites and owns one of the largest pharmaceutical manufacture-owned warehousing and distribution centres in the UK. The company has also invested significantly in increasing its commercial infrastructure worldwide and manages its own logistics, regulatory, intellectual property and marketing requirements in the regions of operations. The company produces large batches of common pharmaceutical products in its European manufacturing facilities and then transfers them as undifferentiated products that are ready to pack upon requirement in any of the 27 European nations, thereby significantly saving time in supply-chain movement.

The company has nearly 7000 product approvals in Europe and has a marketing portfolio of over 400 molecules across multiple therapeutic classes including Oncology, Cardiology, Neurology, Nephrology, Urology, Diabetology, Pain management and Gastroenterology. The company has also forayed into the development of biosimilar and new chemical entities.

Accord Healthcare has been focusing on delivering high-quality affordable medicines and has developed strong in-house capabilities through global partnering, in-licensing, out-licensing and co-marketing. Under in-licensing, the company has used business models including straight product supply, technology transfer and co-development. The company has been also offering the hospital or institutional setting service and has witnessed significant growth in this segment during the current pandemic situation.

The company has been the recipient of Global Generics and Bio-similar award in the year 2020 in three categories: Company of the Year, Regulatory Achievement and Corporate Social Responsibility initiatives.

As per Grant Thornton-CII India Meets Britain tracker reports, Accord Healthcare (UK) has the distinction of being one of very few Indian investing companies in the UK that performed exceedingly well in UK for eight consecutive years (2013–14 to 2019–20) on the parameter of turnover performance. The company had more than ten per cent turnover growth for several years which itself is a distinction in a difficult and competitive UK market. The turnover of Accord Healthcare (UK) in the eight-year period starting from 2012–13 to 2019–20 is reflected in Figure 5.8.

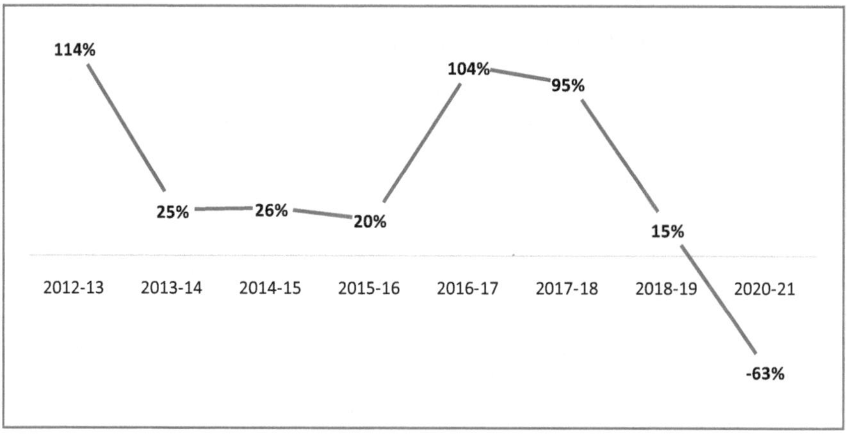

Figure 5.8 Turnover growth – Accord Healthcare (the UK), 2012–2020

Source: Accord Healthcare Limited, Company information. Retrieved September 25, 2021 from www.uk.globaldatabase.com/company/accord-healthcare-limited and Accord Healthcare filing history, UK Government. Retrieved September 21, 2021, from www.find-and-update.company-information.service.gov.uk/company/04596349/filing-history

Reasons for investment in the UK by Accord Healthcare

Accord Healthcare has used the strategy to operate from the UK for entry to EU markets. The company also recognized the local market opportunities in the UK in the bulk drug segment and has been responsible for around 20% of UK's generic pharmaceutical prescriptions in the year 2019–20. The company has been able to obtain 7,000 product approvals in Europe and has marketing portfolio of over 400 molecules across multiple therapeutic classes because of its organic and inorganic growth in the UK and other global markets. The company also has been able to build robust research and development capabilities because of its UK market presence and skilled human resource.

Impact of Brexit and COVID-19 on Accord Healthcare

The company is impacted because of Brexit and has experienced a fall in its turnover due to a change in supply routes to respective EMENA companies by the parent company Intas Pharmaceuticals.

COVID-19 has also impacted the business performance to some extent. However, in view of the pandemic, the company has geared up quickly and worked closely with UK and EU governments and agencies for ensuring that critical medicines are made available to the patients in the region. The company has been also offering the hospital or institutional setting service and has witnessed significant growth in this segment during the current pandemic situation.

In years to come, the company will have to take strategic view on the impact of Brexit on its inroads to EU markets through the UK. The relocation of European MHRA (European Medicine and Healthcare Product Regulatory Agency) from the UK will have an impact on the long-term strategic decisions of the company.

Case Study 3: HCL Technologies (the UK)

HCL Technologies is a leading IT service-providing Indian company in the UK since 1997. HCL has been offering its service and products through three business units of IT and Business Services (ITBS), Engineering and Research and Development Services (ERS) and Products and Platforms (P&P). The ITBS assists the global firms to transform their business operations through digital applications, IT infrastructure, digital process operations and digital transformation solutions. ERS offers digital engineering services and solutions in various aspects of product development and platform engineering. P&P provides customized software products to the global clients for their specific technology and industry requirements. HCL Technologies is offering its products and services across various industry verticals in Financial services, Manufacturing, Telecom and Media, Retail, Life Sciences and Healthcare, Entertainment, Oil and Gas, Energy, Travel and Transportation, and Public services.

The company also has FinTech Innovation Lab in London. Its customers include Fortune 500 and Fortune 1000 companies from the UK and globally.

HCL UK operations employs more than 2,500 people for supporting 50+ clients in the European region. The company has been effectively and efficiently building digital talent pool in the European region and has been accorded the recognition of being one of the top employers in the UK for last several years by the Top Employers Institute. The institute identifies the employers that provide highest standards in employee conditions and also nurtures talent. HCL (the UK) has a unique ideapreneurship programme that provides employees with opportunity to innovate and collaborate with each other and with the customers to solve business problems and fosters grassroots innovation. The employees can use the HCL idea sharing and collaborating platforms and formats like Value Portal, Mad Jams, Good Practices Conference (GPC) and Intellectual Property Monetization (IPM) for innovation and collaboration within the organization. The concept is based on the belief that inversion of the organization pyramid leads to innovation, engagement and empowerment of the front-line employees who are directly connected with the customers.

The company has also been the recipient of recognition in other categories like being top performer in the IT Service Provider category for delivering value and excellence in its outsourcing partnerships (GSA UK 2018 award). The company also has been offering next-generation workplace solutions for transforming workplaces into customized, collaborative, connected, innovative and intelligent workspaces and has been recognized as a leading firm for the Gartner 'Managed Workplace Services in Europe' in the year 2017.

The company, in May 2021, has announced expansion of its investment in the UK with hiring of a thousand technology professionals to support clients in UK and worldwide in areas of digital transformation, cloud and artificial intelligence.

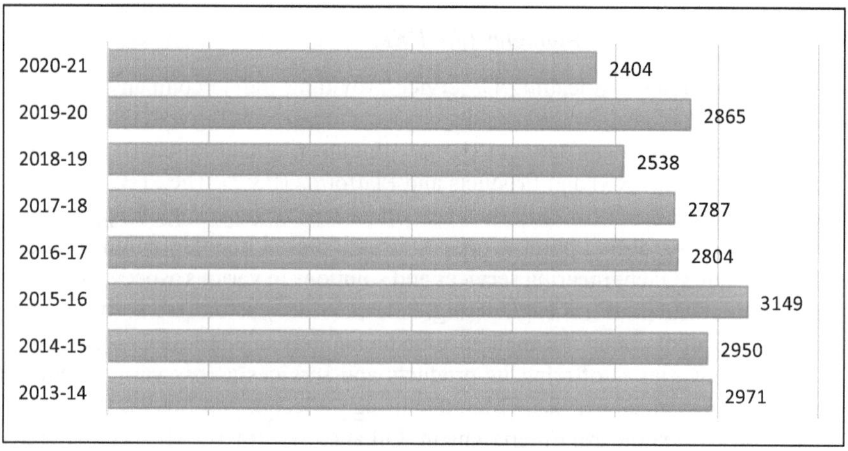

Figure 5.9 Year-wise number of local employees in HCL Technologies UK operations, 2014–2021

Source: Grant Thornton-CII India Meets Britain tracker (various years).

The HCL Technologies' (UK) performance has been phenomenal because of two reasons. One has been that the company has consistently hired and used the local IT talent in the UK to the best of its advantage thereby leveraging its growth and second because of continuous growth in its turnover including in the pandemic hit year of 2020–21. As per Grant Thornton-CII report, the turnover of HCL technologies (UK) grew at the rate of 24% in the year 2020–21.

Reasons for investment in the UK by HCL Technologies

HCL Technologies also has used the strategy to operate from the UK for entry to the EU markets. The company had also recognized the local market opportunities in the technology sector in the UK and hence has local talent pool for offering its service and products through business units of IT and Business Services, Engineering and Research and Development Services and Products and Platforms. HCL Technologies (UK) has effectively used the UK and EU market opportunities by leveraging the digital economy and digital infrastructure and local talent pool in the region.

Impact of Brexit and COVID-19 on HCL Technologies

The company has not been impacted much by Brexit. The hiring of local talent and exploration of market opportunities in the region due to Brexit have enhanced the growth of the company. The movement to new custom and legal procedures has created a new opportunity for business in the UK for HCL. Similarly, the COVID-19 pandemic has offered additional opportunities for business in the region because of rising demand for online products and platforms and IT solutions.

Case Study 4: Jaguar Land Rover Automotive Plc

Tata Motors acquired the iconic brands Jaguar and Land Rover in 2008 for USD 2.3 billion. Both the brands merged under one company Jaguar Land Rover Automotive Plc in the year 2013. Jaguar has a range of luxury sedans, sports cars and luxury-performance SUVs. On the other hand, the Land Rover has a portfolio of premium all-terrain vehicles.

This acquisition has provided Tata Motors an opportunity to enter in a big league of global automakers. The acquired brands carry a strong premium connect worldwide. The quality global processes and best practices of the two global brands have also offered great learning in building the domestic car brands in the portfolio of Tata Motors. The Tata Motors domestic automotive production capabilities have improved, leading to higher success rate of new domestic car launches by Tata Motors. The company has several manufacturing facilities in the UK. The company also has manufacturing joint venture in China. The company has also started its manufacturing facility in Nitra, Slovakia, in 2018 and has contract manufacturing in Austria and local assembly operations

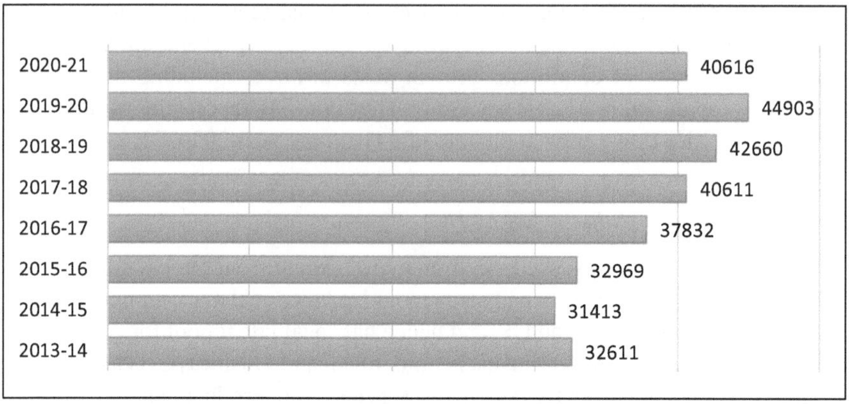

Figure 5.10 Year-wise number of local employees in JLR operations, 2014–2021
Source: Grant Thornton-CII India Meets Britain tracker (various years).

in Brazil and India. In the ten-year period, since the acquisition, the sales of JLR increased from being less than 2,00,000 units a year to more than 6,00,000 units per year. The company moved to profit position by the year 2010 from its previous loss-making position at the time of acquisition in the year 2008. The company in the recent years has also received several awards for engineering excellence, automotive technologies and innovative design. Fresh investment of GBP 3.8 billion was made in new automotive technologies, research and development in the 'Autonomous, Connected, Electric and Shared' (ACES) Strategy in the FY2019.

The company is also the largest employer of local human resource in the UK. Figure 5.10 represents the employee numbers of JLR over last eight years in the UK starting from the year 2013–14 to the year 2020–21.

The company has recently announced its 're-imagine' strategy under which it is planning Jaguar as an all-electric luxury by the year 2025, and similarly the Land Rover will introduce six pure electric variants in next five years and first all-electric Land Rover model in 2024. The company is aiming at net zero carbon emissions across all supply chain and product operations by 2039.

In short term, the company is looking at the adoption of clean fuel-cell power in line with hydrogen economy within next twelve months. However, according to some analysts, the re-imagining strategy is a delayed decision and that the company, in recent years, has been slow in making forays in electric vehicles and related innovation, while its competitors have moved ahead in the said segment. This may impact the competitive business efficiency of the company in the years to come. It is a well-known fact that in the automotive sector, brand positioning is becoming challenging day by day because of intense competition and disruptive technologies.

Reasons for investment in Jaguar and Land Rover Brands by Tata Motors

Britain has been the home to several world-class iconic brands, and this has accentuated the interest of Indian companies in the UK. Several acquisition deals by Tata group including the acquisition of Jaguar and Land Rover brand were done with the reason of gaining access to the international premium automotive markets. The purpose of JLR acquisition was also to get access to the cutting-edge engineering practices, technical know-how, intellectual property and the research and development capabilities. The acquisitions made by Tata Motors were driven by the engineering and design capabilities of the UK brands and for creating the mutually beneficial relationship thereby building even the domestic Tata Motors brand.

Impact of Brexit and COVID-19 on Jaguar and Land Rover

JLR had recovered from the loss-making performance in the year 2010, post completion of the Jaguar and Land Rover acquisition by Tata Motors in the year 2008, and had again registered pre-tax and post-tax losses in the years 2018–19 and 2019–20 and 2020–21. According to the company, it was impacted by Brexit concerns influencing its sales in the region and worldwide. Though a new trade agreement has been reached between the UK and EU in December 2020, the friction in the process of new custom administration and documentation continue to impact the business as well as connect with the suppliers. The production operations of the company have also been disrupted in the UK because of semiconductor shortage worldwide in the premium automotive segment. The production in two of the UK plants was halted due to the supply disruptions because of semiconductor shortage in the first half of 2021. COVID-19 had also resulted in fall in demand and drop in the product sales of the JLR worldwide.

Overall impact of Brexit and COVID-19 on Indian investing companies in the UK

There have been several advantages of investing in Britain. These advantages are not going away due to Brexit. Hence, the Indian companies will continue to make UK-targeted investments in sectors like Technology, Engineering, Financial Services, Automotive, Energy and Media. On the other hand, some sectors that are impacted are Pharmaceuticals and Chemicals, Technology and Telecom Manufacturing companies that had considered the UK as gateway to the EU. Figure 5.11 captures the reasons for continued Indian investment in the UK despite Brexit as well as the reasons for negative impact of Brexit on some sectors.

COVID-19 pandemic, on the other hand, has impacted companies worldwide. Barring few companies in sectors like pharmaceuticals and technology, all Indian companies that had invested in the UK have faced downturn in their sales turnover and profit performance. Impact of pandemic is short term, and long-term

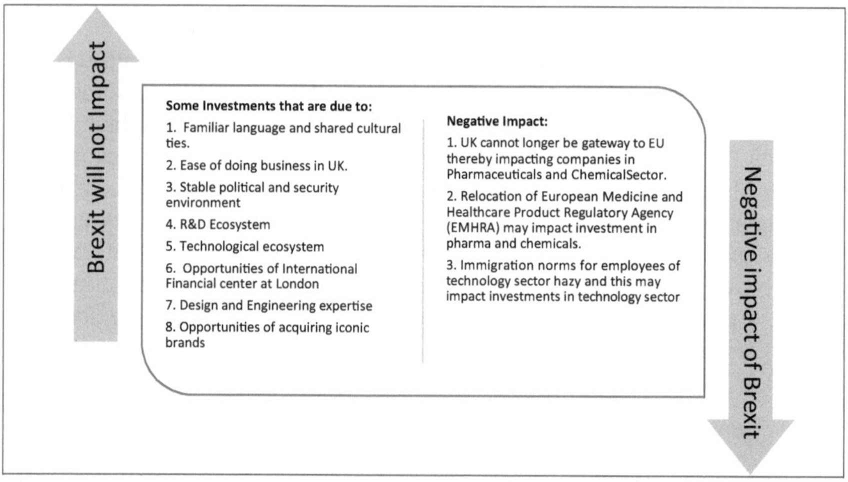

Figure 5.11 Overall impact of Brexit on Indian investments in the UK

Source: 'India Meets Britain' tracker reports of Grant Thornton-CII (various years) and other industry and media reports.

growth in Indian investments in the UK will be enhanced with enhanced economic recovery of India and the UK. Governments and related agencies in the two countries are already working in various ways to smoothen out the negative impact of Brexit and COVID-19 pandemic on business operations. UK government has announced that India will be a priority country for setting bilateral FTA (Free Trade Agreement). Bilateral trade and investment groups are working to smoothen trade and investments in many business areas. New trade deal between the UK and the EU has offered some clarity on the norms of export and trade in goods between the two regions though the same has led to new custom norms and increased paperwork. The Indian companies in the sectors like Pharma and Chemicals etc., are exploring the bonded warehouses to avoid double tariffs on the passage of goods through the UK to Europe. The UK's point-based immigration system has also created more opportunities for Indians to work in the UK. The UK has also relaxed work opportunity norms for the foreign students graduating from UK higher education institutions.

Most important factor in the UK–India relationship has been the enthusiasm and positivity exhibited by top political executives in the two countries to strengthen trade and investment ties between the two countries. Hence, India in the financial year 2020–21 was the second largest source country for FDI projects in the UK (inward), and the UK has continued to be one of the largest investing nations in India.

6 Trade and investment between India and Visegrad Group

Prana Krishna Biswas and Robert Dygas

Introduction

Visegrad Group (V4) has its 30th year of anniversary in 2021 since its inception in 1991 when Czechoslovakia's President Václav Havel had put the hand-written draft of Visegrad Declaration in Visegrad, Hungary. This is a long perspective enough to see how this group developed after collapse of Soviet Union and what was the main achievement regarding trade and investment. The main success was the unification of V4 members Poland, Czech Republic, Slovakia and Hungary. Today, there are some tensions between Poland and Czech Republic regarding the compensations for Czech Republic due to environmental problems caused by Polish energy plant Turów. The problem is not solved yet, but it shows that even in the similar neighbour countries there are areas of conflict as well. Such aspects are quite important because they may impact future relations. The V4 should not be treated as the EU–V4 division but rather as an economic and political platform for countries which were in Warsaw Pact which was over in 1991. Besides V4 Group, there is another also important initiative called Three Seas (lat. *Trimarium*) Initiative (3SI) launched in 2015 by Polish President Andrzej Duda and Croatian President Kolinda Grabar-Kitarović. That shows that eastern bloc of the EU has lot of potential for the development regarding the trade and investment. Both groups are important although 3SI is much bigger and includes 12 European countries. The main difference between V4 and 3SI is the focus. V4 is focusing more on political relations among the partners, while 3SI shows more focussed approach towards economy. In 2018, the 3SI initiative initiated by Poland was about building infrastructure (highway) across the member countries called via Carpatia which is a route running on the North–South axis between the Baltic, Aegean, Black, and Adriatic Seas. That initiative included countries from V4 (Poland, Slovakia, Hungary) and international partners like Turkey, Greece, Ukraine, and Belarus as well. The overlap of the V4 and 3SI same-member countries may also cause problems to be fully active in each initiative taken. Both V4 and 3SI are getting more attentions of the international investors and are getting recognised as being the tools for strengthening transatlantic and non-European cooperation with such countries like Brazil, India, China, and South Africa (BRICS). There are also "pull" type initiatives from China, for example 17+1 for cooperation with CEE

DOI: 10.4324/9781003274933-6

countries, but it is rather not tailored well to the needs of the V4 and 3SI members (Europeum, 2021). Main reason for that is that China acts on the asymmetric agreements trying to own EU's assets and make the member state countries adjust to the Chinese economic rules. China is also trying to take advantage of the fact that other BRICS countries do not treat V4 as the potential player and valuable partner. V4 Group members evaluated cooperation with China as not beneficial to them due to the fact that the proposed model of cooperation by China was not conforming to the EU standards, and it was financially expensive. China model was mainly based on the mergers and acquisitions of CEE companies which did not result in the creation of new jobs and did not bring more value to V4 Group economies. Poland and Czech Republic had bad experiences with Chinese investments, namely CEFC in energy sector in Czech Republic and COVAC in constructing motorway in Poland. It shows that there are no economic evidences that 17+1 initiative of China is going to last long as the support of the V4 Group for cooperation with China is decreasing even though Hungary is still showing some interest in Chinese investments (Przychodniak, 2020).

It is the time that V4 and 3SI should intensify the cooperation with India to have it as a reliable and strong partner as the counterpart to China. Some explanation taken from the literature should throw a light to better understand the Indian vision of the economic relations and building up the partnerships. In the literature, there is a focus on two dimensions, namely EU–India cooperation and bilateral trade and investment relations between India and chosen EU countries. EU–India relations were presented by some authors based on the Rajendra Jain's observations on the "narrow circles", where in the first circle are France, Germany, and EU institutions (replacing the UK after Brexit), in the second circle are the other EU member states including V4 Group and 3SI countries, and in the third circle, there are some EU member states that have no interest to cooperate with India at all (Aspengren et al., 2021). From an Indian perspective, the EU is the only entity which exists in formal documents for cooperation in Join Action Plan formulated by the Government of India (GoI). The strategic partnerships according to GoI enable the expansion of policy choices and developmental options and assume the understanding and openness on both sides. It also indicates the upgrade of qualitative transformation of mutual interaction and maturing of relationship. India focuses on four objectives in each strategic partnership. The first objective is economical that consist of three elements: (1) increase the potential of trade and investment, (2) market access for Indian products, (3) contribution to Indian growth and development. The second objective is to keep strategic autonomy. The third objective is based on sovereign equality and on comparative advantage and a mutuality of interests and benefits. The fourth objective is a partnership where one side is prescriptive or one side is intrusive, and the other side is, in a sense, a passive partner (Jain, 2014). According to one of the Indian think tanks, a strategic partnership is a long-term interaction between two countries based on political, economic, social, and historical factors (Azad & Gupta, 2011). According to the Foundation for National Security Research (FNSR, 2011), a New-Delhi-based think tank, a strategic partnership should be a new pattern of international relationships in which nations enter into freewheeling partnerships with other nations based on complementarity of interests in specific but vital areas. It does not bind nations to support each other on all strategic issues in all situations. Each partnership has its own character and focuses on certain core areas of national interest such as defence, national security, energy supply, trade and investment, cooperation in science and technology. GoI due to lack of the security and defence dimension in EU–India partnership agreement does not treat it as the "strategic" in the meaning itself. From the other perspective, the lack of the political priority in V4 Group to start direct talks with India can be the serious obstacle. V4 Group is still validated by the European Commission and gets its approval for the strategic initiatives taken. That is why the EU–India strategic agreement is negotiated by the European Commission, and the main roles are performed by Germany and France in the negotiations with India. Strategic partnerships have not proven to be appropriate instruments to promote effective multilateralism, since partners have different perceptions and expectations. There is also a mismatch in perception of global issues by the EU and India. One of such global issue is the dominance of China in European economy, while for India a business opportunity is an important matter. India tries to keep out of the political initiatives led by China, so as an example, India did not join the Regional Comprehensive Economic Partnership in 2020 due to asymmetric economic power and dominance aspiration of China in Indo-Pacific region. Similar approach is followed with the 17+1 initiative which can be seen as the Chinese rivalry in European market against the United States. Another difference in the approach towards relations between India and the EU is that the EU's preference is rather functional and revisionist multilateralism, which should be achievable while India's preference sticks to rather instrumental approach and effective multilateralism with the equality of partners especially in the relations between EU member states (Gratius, 2011). India puts lot of attention to United Nation institutional issues and sustainable development. One of the studies showed that only few EU members managed to engage with India on more than five global issues. The EU members such as the Netherlands, Spain, and Sweden, even though they paid bilateral visits to India on more than average number of occasions, maintained the relations with India through the EU rather than in a direct bilateral way. As the explanation of such approach, Germany and France had the highest number of high-level visits to India during 2014–2019 (Aspengren et al., 2021)

The reason why India is not yet intensifying relations with V4 is because the main Indian foreign direct investments in the EU countries are mainly in Switzerland, the UK, the Netherlands, Germany, and France. India is a huge country with lot of potential, and it was not used so far by Poland and other V4 members to strengthen their economic position (Dygas, 2021). Cooperation with India can be a new agenda for V4 and can be included in V4 presidency programmes. This is one of the roles of V4 to build its position in the EU and start trade and investment cooperation with India. Recent EU–China Investment Agreement from 2020 (CAI) does not help V4 to change the focus from China to India taking into consideration that it was mainly the initiative of Germany to force such agreement and stimulate other member states to approve it. This is still an ongoing process, and V4 together with 3CI can have the influence to change it by inviting more companies from India to invest in V4 countries.

V4 is an interesting group for Foreign Direct Investment (FDI). In 2014, the net inflow of FDI to V4 was 24 billion USD which was 9.4% of FDI inflow of the EU, and 58% of that was generated by Poland (PISM, 2016). V4–India relations were mainly focused on education and economy. There were several visits of V4 prime ministers to India in the last decade. Czech and Hungary were mainly interested in developing mutual relation with India in the military defence and security sectors. In terms of security cooperation, the Czech Republic and India engaged mainly in mutual training activities and education. Hungary supported India to have a seat in UN Security Council. In 2003, India and Hungary signed *The Agreement on Defence Cooperation*, which was reviewed by Indo-Hungarian Joint Defence Committee in 2013 by both countries. On the contrary, Poland was mainly focused on trade and investments with India. There were several visits of the Polish government officials to India, but there was no significant breakthrough result of these visits for developing bilateral relations. This is mainly because Poland has locked itself with China and not elaborated any strategic approach to other Asian countries, especially to India. Poland is not also a strategic partner in trade and investment for India. FDI inflow to Poland between 2000 and 2020 was just 0.15% of total Indian FDI outflow (Dygas, 2021). Slovakia also focused on the good trade and investment relations with India. They signed several documents for mutual cooperation with India, and Agreement on Economic cooperation (2004) and the Agreement on the Promotion and Reciprocal Protection of Investments (2006) were the most significant ones. As it is seen, each V4 member has some relations with India so it is the time for V4 to act together and formulate a new strategy approach with India to off-set the Chinese dominance in Europe now, which can be dangerous from the longer perspective. Each V4 member has a decline in trade in goods with India since 2011, and also the pandemic COVID-19 has been worsening the trade relations. The current trade balance of V4 countries with India for 2020 is presented in the Table 6.1.

Table 6.1 V4–India trade balance in 2020

V4 member	*Trade Balance in Million EUR*
Poland	-739
Hungary	-173
Slovakia	-68
Czech Republic	0

Source: Based on Eurostat 2021, https://ec.europa.eu/eurostat/statistics-explained/index.php?title=File:EU_trade_balance_of_goods_with_India,_2020.png#file, access 08.07.2021

All V4 countries had a negative trade balance with India besides Czech Republic (which had same export and import value) in the trade with India in 2020. To change this situation, V4 together with 3SI should invite India as the partner to new initiatives, especially in the areas of:

(1) investment in *via Carpatia,*
(2) vitalising V4 + British relations in a post-Brexit period
(3) initiative of #GlobalVisegrad, involving new global partners in V4+ consultations: Australia, Central Asia, Pacific Alliance, African Union
(4) enhancing V4 + the USA dialogue
(5) working closely with Japan and South Korea
(6) joint tourism and economic promotion

The main question is how India may be involved to support the aforementioned activities. According to opinion of Mr. Adam Burakowski, the Ambassador of Poland in India, it can be happen when the EU–India partnership agreement (Broad-Based Trade and Investment Agreement) will be finally signed by both parties (Basu, 2021). This is partially right if Poland depends only on this agreement which is under discussions since 2007 to develop its relations with India. Another important fact is that Poland is not the main negotiator of this agreement with India and has very limited influence on that if any. During the last India–EU summit, which was held virtually in July 2020, both sides failed to arrive at a conclusion in reviving the talks that got stuck on issues such as reduction of tariffs and market access. The lack of strategic approach of Poland towards relations with India and the dependency on the readiness of EU agreements make the situation for entire V4 Group uncomfortable. Another question is how V4 Group can restore relations with India if the EU–India talks are not fruitful. One of the workaround solution can be vitalising V4+British relations in a post-Brexit period. The UK is no longer in the EU, and it is restoring very good trade and investment relations with India. Both countries have long history and economic relations which can be the opportunity for V4 Group to access the Indian market. The UK wants to double the value of the trade with India by the 2030 from a current level of 33 billion euros in 2019. This agreement between UK and India is known as "quantum leap" (Mayes, 2021). The UK–EU relations are not amiable after Brexit. Fishing was one of the hard points in the agreement negotiations. The UK protect their waters with Royal Navy patrol ships from EU-fishermen exploring UK's exclusive water zone. Even though there is still an opportunity for V4 and 3SI to restore good trade and investment relations with the UK. The number of V4 citizens still living in the UK makes the situation better for bilateral trade relations between V4 and the UK.

Characteristics of Indian MNCs operating in Visegrad Group region

Over the previous decade, four Visegrad nations, namely Poland, Hungary, Slovak Republic, and Czech Republic (V4), have been among the fastest growing in the European Union. The V4 makes up the twelfth largest economy in the world, worth over 1 trillion USD, which is over one-third of India's size, and offers a consumer market of 64 million inhabitants, which is 12.5% of the EU's total investment. India's export to EU member countries stood at about USD 54 billion in 2019–20, while import aggregated to 52 billion USD. V4's trade with India as of US$4 billion (S$5.56 billion in 2018) is far below the potential level. While the V4's shares in the EU's external exports stood at 10.1 per cent in 2016, its share in the EU's exports to India was only 3.6%. Similarly, while they count for 9.6% of the total EU imports, in the case of India it was only half of that proportion at 5.6% of EU's imports from India in 2016. As these V4 countries, which are heavily dependent on the European market, are searching for new economic partners beyond Europe, India seems to be an attractive destination. With a long tradition of cooperation in Indian industrialization from the 1960s–80s, they offer new and low-cost technologies today in areas required for Indian modernization programs, from infrastructure to sanitation and agro-processing. Not many Indians are aware that companies that are already well-established in India, like Bata, Bella India, Home Credit and Skoda, are from the V4 region. Also, Indian firms like Infosys and Tata have major investments in the V4. The region has already become a new destination for Indian tourists and a place for the growing Indian diaspora. With one of the lowest unemployment levels across Europe, they may soon become even more amicable to migrants from Asia, as per the recent decision by the Czech Republic to grant 500 high-skill long stay visas to Indian professionals. India shows the interest of cooperation with each of V4 member especially in military and security sectors.

Strong defence connections exist between India and Czech Republic. The Agreement on Defence Cooperation between India and the Czech Republic was signed in October 2007, but this was also the only year when a bilateral action plan of cooperation was set up. A Czech–Indian Commission for Defence Cooperation is also in place, but its last session took place in September 2011. At the international level, the Czech Republic supports India's ambitions to become a permanent member of the UN Security Council and overall reform of the UN. India and the Czech Republic are boosting ties in the defence sector, with New Delhi's invitation to Prague defence companies for setting up joint ventures as a crucial partner in next-generation technology. In addition, a contract was signed by Czech-based PBS to produce aircraft engines in India in 2020. It must be noted, however, that India's military inventory is in a large part composed of Russian systems and weapons, which may not always be compatible with Czech defence industry products. Nevertheless, the defence industry represents one of the biggest potentials for Czech exports to India with New Delhi increasing allocations to its military budget. In terms of security cooperation, the Czech Republic and India engage mainly in mutual training activities and education. The Czech Republic offers India training in its CBRN facilities and the possibility to organise CIED training in tandem. Prominent Indian companies across various sectors now have a footprint in the Czech Republic. Some examples being Infosys, Ashok Leyland, Glenmark Pharmaceuticals, and Lloyd Electric and

Engineering Ltd. Some years back in 2011, the Czech government had already identified India among 12 priority countries for the promotion of mutual commercial, investment, and other economic activities. India–Czech bilateral trade stands currently at 1.6 billion USD.

Hungary also emerged as being one of the first countries from the Warsaw Pact, which emphasised political and business relations with India. However, efforts to intensify trade ties failed on many occasions. It was only after the economic liberalisation in India and democratic transition in Hungary that the two partners' trade linkages witnessed a surge. New Delhi–Budapest trade ties continue to witness an upward trajectory (pegged at 750 million USD in 2020), and Indian companies like TCS, Genpact, Sun Pharma, Crompton Greaves, SMR, and Orion are prominent investors in Hungary. Between 2014 and 2015, Apollo Tyres and SMP-Group were also the largest investors in Hungary's greenfield projects. Two Indian companies, Apollo Tyres and SMP-Group, carried out the largest green field investments in Hungary in 2014 and 2015. The Sona Group, an established components' manufacturer for the automotive industry, launched a 4.2 billion HUF project to build a new manufacturing plant in Polgár, Hajdú-Bihar county, in Hungary, creating more new jobs.

As far as Poland is concerned, there is a huge potential in enhancing the business relationship between India and Poland, which is waiting to be tapped. But this can only be done when India and the EU sign the trade pact, which has been under discussion since 2007. BTIA–EU India FTA agreement has been under discussion for many years now. This will make the lives of Indian companies and traders easier. Going forward, there are new areas of cooperation that can boost the overall trade ties between India and Poland. These areas include corporate finance and IT services, food and agro-processing technologies, renewable energy, cybersecurity, FinTech, etc. In addition, Punjab–Lubelskie, Andhra Pradesh–Małopolska, and Maharashtra–Wielkopolska are some of the prominent examples of sub regional cooperation between India and Poland. Not to mention, India and Poland share strong linkages on the international stage. It was Poland that sponsored the UNSC Resolution 1267 [2019] to impose a ban on Jaish-e-Mohammad. Similarly, Poland showed unequivocal support for India's position on Kashmir post the abrogation of Article 370. Poland is already India's top commercial partner in Central Europe. Though commerce between the two nations has increased sevenfold in the previous 10 years, reaching over 3 billion USD in 2017, this does not represent the size of the two economies.

Among the V4, India's connect with Slovakia is relatively slow paced. Slovakia has a strong presence in the car industry, electronics, and heavy machinery. These could be prospective areas of interest for India. Indian investments are now gradually moving to Slovakia with a huge contribution by Tata in the automotive sector. Investment of the Jaguar Land Rover has been finalized, bringing the largest Indian-owned personal car plant in Europe. Slovakia has also signed a MoU for cooperation with the Indian Ministry of Railways. This fits in well with the Government of India's "Make in India" initiative and has opened up a large area for cooperation, including producing coaches for trains and modernisation of rail systems, including software and hardware. The case study of Tata Motors investment in Slovakia is presented in section 6.3 of this chapter.

Tata Motors case study from Slovakia

Jaguar Land Rover (JLR) plant was opened in Slovakia on 25 October 2018 with an investment of 1.4 billion euros made by the Tata Motors, which is a pure Indian company with annual capacity of 150 000 cars. Originally JLR was British, but it was bought by Tata Motors in 2008 (M&A type of the investment) and before that time in the past JLR was in financial troubles after a short merger episode with Ford automotive company. Since 2009, Tata Motors implemented a financial reform of the company which helped to focus on the new strategy for the further development and choice of the country for the new plant (Wyles et al., 2013). Since Tata's acquisition, JLR has gone through a significant development process. The company has managed to create a strong brand image and increase its popularity across the key markets (Brazil, China, the UK, India, Austria). JLR has heavily invested in R&D, which is crucial for each car manufacturer if they wish to remain competitive. Thanks to the increasing sales and overall success, JLR started to expand its international activities and managed to launch several new production facilities across the globe (Bhasin, 2018). It was a strategic choice which country to choose for the new plant. The choice was tough as Poland and Slovakia seemed to be preferable options over Mexico and the United States. There were two projects related to that choice. The project called "Oak" was related to the US market, and "Darwin" analysed CEE market. Slovakia was finally chosen as it is a well-known country for automotive industry in CEE region and also a top player as the car producer in Visegrad Group and also a part of automotive cluster with well-established supplier network (Jeakins, 2015). One of Slovakia's advantages over the other countries in V4 was that it belongs to Eurozone which helps to project the cash-flow for the potential investors. Another strong point for placing the investment of Tata Motors in Slovakia was the technology environment especially transforming FDI into technology transfer. It is worthwhile to underline that tax incentives also played a significant role in choosing Slovakia over other countries. Besides that, a new investment of Tata Motors was supported by the EU which helped with a financial aid of 125 million EUR, which helped to keep that investment in the EU instead of moving it to Mexico or the United States.[1] Brexit was also a supportive factor with the choice of plant location in the EU. Those factors helped to make the investment decision, but it did not mean that it was easy and the investment project was out of challenges. The path of that investment of Tata Motors in Slovakia was quite rough for an Indian company as it should have resolved couple of obstacles. The first one was a world competition as many countries such as Mexico, Poland, Hungary, and the United States were ready for the contract with Tata Motors. Moreover, from a macroeconomic perspective, Slovakia was on the downtrend regarding received FDIs during 2009–20014 with an FDI of 2.1% of GDP (Dettoni, 2016). Another problem which needed to be solved was a land for the building the plant (roughly the land of 444 acres was required). Another issue was to secure a trained and skilled human capital. Nitra plant required 2800 employees, while the city of Nitra itself had 85,000. That is why Slovakian government tried to offer the incentives' schemes for those citizens who would move to Nitra to work in the plant. It also included Slovakian citizens working abroad which had been estimated at 200000 workers. As the first in Europe, the plant uses Kuka's Pulse carrier system with over 30% faster transfer times. Jaguar Land Rover currently employs around 1,500 people in Nitra, of which 98% are Slovak nationals and 30% are women. The plant incorporates cutting-edge technologies, and it is the first in Europe to use Kuka's Pulse carrier system with 30% faster transfer times than conventional conveyance systems. It also features a highly automated paint shop process to ensure the highest quality and minimise the environment impact. With an established network of suppliers in close proximity, Jaguar Land Rover has sourced and localised a number of components, such as seats and wheels, to support the production of the Land Rover Discovery in Nitra delivering several thousand additional jobs in the automotive supply chain in Slovakia. All manufacturing employees have taken part in a bespoke 12-week training programme in the company's first overseas training academy, representing an investment of 7.5 million euros. Jaguar Land Rover works closely with the communities near to its manufacturing plants around the world. In the last six months, Jaguar Land Rover has delivered almost 500 volunteering hours to projects in Nitra and surrounding communities; launched its first employee grant programme supporting 12 local projects, including Nitra's first therapeutic sensory room; and most recently has opened a new endowment fund, in conjunction with the Pontis Foundation, to support local projects in the future. Over the course of the last three years, Jaguar Land Rover has delivered new education programmes to inspire the next generation of automotive engineers in Slovakia.

Looking towards the future, the factory will be designed with the flexibility to enable smart, connected manufacturing technologies, such as shop floor visualisation, by using real-time data to solve issues which will support improved process efficiency, delivery, and quality. From 2020, all new Jaguar Land Rover vehicles were electrified, giving the customers even more choice. The major problem which prevails now during COVID-19 in Nitra JLR factory is the demand for chips and semiconductors from China. The issues with components' delivery caused car production suspension in many countries including Slovakia.

Conclusions and way forward

Based on the analysed material, case study of Land Rover in Slovakia, and data given in sections 6.1–6.3 regarding trade and investment relations between India and Visegrad Group, we may conclude that there is still vast unutilised opportunity of Indian economy potential by Visegrad Group countries for strengthening bilateral trade and investment relations with India. Too much focus was put on China and its 17+1 initiative which did not bring any value to V4 countries' development but disintegrated V4 and 3SI cooperation with other Asian countries like India and Japan which indirectly impacted Euro-Atlantic cooperation as well. There are differences in strategic partnership perceptions both between India and EU institution sides and between India and V4+3SI sides. India is putting more interest to cooperate with chosen countries in the second circle (with V4+3SI countries) and not only with the first circle (with Germany, France, EU institutions). The main problem with building the trade and investment relations between India and V4 Group countries is that still EU institutions are the intermediary, and there is limited space for V4+3SI to interact with India directly. This is a problem of the autonomy of the EU member states, working on the strategic partnership agreement with India together with the EU institutions, which should have rather a facilitator instead of the main negotiator role in the entire process. Additionally, the meaning of the word "strategic" in the agreement without defence and national security aspects is making the entire agreement of less value for India. Besides that, the EU is trying to force other investment agreements with China (CAI), which can have negative impacts on investment cooperation with other Asian countries including India. V4 has the bright idea to work and cooperate with everyone (Global Visegrad Initiative), but it needs to be restated as long as the main focus is still on China. It also builds the barrier to enhancing V4+ the USA dialogue.

India has a different strategy and focus, which concentrate on creating "self-reliant economy" (in Hindi it is, *Aatmanirbhar Bharat*). Indian companies need to make profit to survive on the market and are not in the position to get any anti-COVID-19 shield as in the EU even though the COVID-19 Delta was much more severe in India in 2021 than in EU countries. Instead of providing monetary relief directly to Indian companies, Government of India to boost the Indian economy and improving Easy of Doing Business index in the country introduced trade and commerce measures, sectoral reliefs measures, and triggered the stimulus to banking, financial and insurance sector (BSFI) (SIRU, 2020). The way forward is to have an EU–India decent partnership agreement that allows both sides to develop trade and investment relations with respect to the culture and values. EU–India connectivity partnership builds on earlier bilateral agreements, such as the recent "EU-India Strategic Partnership: A Roadmap for 2025" (July 2020), and connects to the wider European policy in the region, as envisioned in the EU Indo-Pacific policy announced in April 2021. Shared values of "democracy, freedom, rule of law, and respect for human rights" underpin EU–India connectivity collaboration, as do operational standards of transparency, viability, inclusiveness, and durability. The first aspect that will determine the success of the EU–India connectivity partnership is the EU's present capacity to implement the initiative's different parts. The European Commission has moved to combine all current financing instruments for operation into one budgetary mechanism known as the "Neighbourhood, Development, and International Cooperation Instrument" (NDICI), to which it has allocated 79.5 billion euros from the years of 2021 to 2027 to reduce the Union's chronic institutional redundancy. For international development projects in Asia and the Indo-Pacific region, 8.49 billion euros would be made available. The NDICI is a big step forward for the European connectivity agenda, not only for its 12% increase in size over the previous year, but also because it is intended to make administration and execution of EU-led projects considerably easier. The NDICI also includes financial assurances to third-party investors, whether institutional or private, such as the European Investment Bank (EIB).

Note

1 For more information, please see https://ec.europa.eu/commission/presscorner/detail/en/IP_18_6023

7 Investment strategies of Chinese platforms in Europe, Tencent case study

Kai Jia and Martin Kenney

Introduction

During the last approximately 18 months, there have been significant macro-political events. First and foremost, the trade war with the United States has grown in intensity. Regulatory uncertainty had already affected global investments and transactions. More recently, the Chinese government has dramatically shifted its stance towards its platform firms within which there will be far more regulatory oversight (McKnight et al., 2021). While the emergence of this new regulatory regime is still underway, it already appears to be having an impact as Chinese platform business groups (PBGs) are reconsidering their domestic businesses and their overseas investment strategies. This chapter explores the reactions of one of China's two largest PBGs, Tencent, to this rapidly evolving environment. Chinese firms have developed an industrial structure, alternative to that of the US West Coast firms (Jia & Kenney, 2021). This PBG model evolved in the unique Chinese market and regulatory environment. However, given the unique character of the model, Chinese firms have found it difficult to achieve significant traction overseas with the possible exception of Southeast Asia where, using joint ventures and acquisitions, Chinese firms have had significant success (Jia et al., 2018). More recently, there have been exceptions; in particular, the global success of TikTok suggests that their previous inability to appeal to consumers outside Asia may be changing.

One of the most important reasons for the rise of the PBG model in China is the loose domestic regulatory environments where mergers, acquisitions, subsidies, etc., are largely tolerated. However, since 2020, as China intensified its regulatory burden on online platforms, whether the PBG model would remain unchanged or be modified becomes a new question. Additionally, the regulatory changes in the domestic market are affecting the Chinese online giants' global expansion strategies. Tencent is an iconic example. According to Refinitiv, for the first six months of 2021, Tencent has consummated a record of 16 deals in Europe and 34 globally in sectors such as social media, gaming, and FinTech. This is compared with four overseas deals in the same period in 2020 and three in 2019 (Ruehl & Riordan, 2021). Similarly, Niko Partners reported that Tencent has closed 51 video game-related deals as of 10 May 2021, of which 39 were domestic companies

DOI: 10.4324/9781003274933-7

and 12 were foreign. The total number is already greater than the 31 deals closed in the whole of 2020 and over five times more than the number closed in 2019. More interestingly, none of the 2021 Tencent investments is located in the United States, while Europe and Southeast Asia are now the main targets (Niko, 2021).

The domestic regulatory change and global expansion strategy transition of Tencent provide some insight into how the PBG model might evolve in the new geopolitical and regulatory environment. This will also provide insight into how Chinese platform firms are reacting to a changing domestic and global political economy. Additionally, given the tensions between the United States and China, how the geographic investments would be affected because of the expansion strategy shifts? The chapter would discuss these questions using the case study of Tencent.

This chapter is organized as follows. The Section 7.2 describes the Chinese platform economy and the emergence of the PBG model. Section 7.3 describes the recent changes in the Chinese regulatory regime and its impact on Tencent's key businesses in FinTech, games, and social networking. Section 7.4 briefly describes some of the recent changes in Tencent's global expansion strategy and compares this with previous strategies. In the concluding discussion in section 7.5, the implications of these changes in terms of global expansion and the development of the PBG model are explored.

Contexts for Chinese platform economy: the heterogeneity of online platforms

The platform economy is now impacting countries and businesses globally (Nambisan et al., 2019). The general tendency has been to focus on the supposed universal characteristics, nearly all of which were drawn entirely from the US experience and, in particular, the Silicon Valley ideology (Kenney & Zysman, 2020). Previous research on platform characteristics is drawn from a long-standing tradition in economics that identified the following features of successful platforms, which suggested that they exhibited the following phenomena: lock-ins (Arthur, 1989), winner-take-all markets (Arthur, 1996), network effects (Parker & Van Alstyne, 2005), long-tail distributions (Brynjolfsson et al., 2006), etc. While these characteristics are not exclusive online platforms, they seem to exhibit the outcomes of these markets. More specific research on online platforms has remarked upon how they organize multisided structures (Rochet & Tirole, 2006) and exhibit a modular architecture (Baldwin & Woodard, 2009) that requires the provision and management of boundary resources. These studies have explored intra- and inter-platform competition dynamics (Gawer, 2014; Eisenmann et al., 2011), as well as the platform's growth and expansion strategies (Aversa et al., 2020; Hagiu, 2009).

Because of the dominance of the US West Coast online platform firms, until very recently, researchers have largely ignored the fact that different political economies might be able to generate varieties of platform economic arrangements (Wang & Coe, 2021). The lack of attention to the impacts of political context on online platformization has been hypothesized to be related to the scientific management approach since the 1950s (Van Tulder Et Al., 2016). Focusing on factors like firm-specific capacity, market mechanisms, and industrial architecture, management researchers overlooked the political economic factors that might cause differences in the platform structures and strategies. As we indicated previously, the Chinese case shows that a global-class industry with quite different organizational characteristics could emerge (Jia & Kenney, 2021). Globally, five platform firms, Amazon, Apple, Facebook, Google, and Microsoft, appear to have achieved dominance. Chinese online platform leaders, Alibaba and Tencent, were, until the Chinese government's crackdown on platform giants in 2021, also listed in the world's ten most valuable firms due to the remarkable power in the Chinese economy. Alibaba, Tencent, and the other Chinese platform firms have been developing global-class competencies in a number of software-based and other online technologies. Given the enormous market, online platforms in China were confronted with a different political economic context within which they could evolve and develop competencies. However, only a few thus far, such as Tiktok and Shein, have been adopted by consumers outside of China. In other words, though the US West Coast model was not the sole way of organizing the platform economy (Kenney & Zysman, 2016, 2020), until recently, it was the undisputed dominant one.

Platform business group model of Chinese online platforms

Business groups are "firms which though legally independent, are bound together by a constellation of formal and informal ties and are accustomed to take coordinated action" (Khanna & Rivkin, 2001). Of course, business groups are not a new organizational form and have been common in emerging economies. They are composed of a population of firms that are independent but linked together through equity holdings, cross-marketing their various products, purchasing from each other, and directing commerce to their various constituent members. The difference between a platform business group (PBG) and traditional business groups is that the platform firm is the linchpin and not, as in the case of the Japanese keiretsu, the main bank. Moreover, though there are a few exceptions, the cross-holdings are not a network with each of the firms in the PBG owning stock in the others but rather a hub-and-spoke design with the platform firm having bilateral relations with other members (there are a few exceptions such as JD.com, Tencent, and VIP shop's arrangement). These online firms created the PBG model because of the unique problems they faced in the domestic market (Jia & Kenney, 2021).

In contrast to the US online platforms that only used acquisitions and organic expansions as a growth model, Chinese firms developed two other expansion strategies: joint stock cross-holding arrangements with other internet and non-internet firms and spinning-off divisions through the sale of partial ownership in public or private markets – the classic case of this was Alibaba's failed spinoff and listing of its financial operations, Ant Financial. In addition, the Chinese platform giants used open source software, commoditizing the operating system and introducing higher-level services, such as super apps and payment services that they leveraged to privilege their PBG partners.

Regulatory contexts and Chinese platforms' global expansion

The differences between Chinese online giants and those in the United States highlighted the neglected importance of political economic context in framing the structure and strategy of online platforms. Despite the extremely rich ecosystems of the PBG model in the domestic market, Chinese online giants still have much difficulty expanding globally.

One of the critical reasons to explain the rise of the PBG model of Chinese platform firms was the loose domestic regulatory environment (Jia & Kenney, 2021). Clearly, US firms expanded horizontally and channelled traffic; there were regulatory limits. Moreover, the structure of the PBG model has proven to be difficult to export. The great Chinese overseas successes, TikTok and Shein, did not even try to export the PBG model globally. The US platform giants are built based upon controlling layers in the stack to capture value from the entire industry, like Google owning Android while Apple benefits from the AppStore (Kenney & Pon, 2011) or vertical applications such as Search. The Chinese online giants had lacked the bottlenecks in the stack that their US analogues had developed, thereby making it challenging for them to compete in the global market. In contrast, they developed "killer" services such as Alipay or WeChat that became their own bottleneck services. However, due to the nature of these applications, their customer base was largely confined to the domestic market. Given the huge scale of the Chinese market, they could still enjoy impressive growth that during the early period may have impeded their motivation to go abroad. For example, after a series of unsuccessful globalization efforts, Baidu finally withdrew its overseas operations to concentrate on the domestic market ever since.

However, the rise of the platform economy has triggered regulatory responses globally (Cioffi et al., 2021; Van Dijck et al., 2018). Influenced by Karl Polanyi's concept of the double movement, societies globally are reacting to the power of the platforms and thus the domestic environments for which platforms are evolving (Kenney et al., 2020). This tendency has also affected China. Therefore, the impact of the domestic regulatory environment change on the globalization strategy of Chinese online platforms is interesting to explore.

Regulatory change in China

The Chinese government was considered to be a loose regulator concerning online firms. Not only were mergers between leading companies broadly permitted, but also there were rarely anti-trust or anti-unfair-competition investigations against online platforms. One milestone case illustrating the relatively weak position of regulators was the disputes between the State Administration for Industry and Commerce (SAIC) and Alibaba at the very beginning of 2015.

The SAIC announced that in a sampling inspection, 63% of the products sold on Alibaba's online Taobao marketplace were found to be "inauthentic", meaning they were fake, discredited, or came through unauthorized channels. However, Taobao responded to the SAIC, questioning the validity of the sampling methods. In response to the accusations, the SAIC released a white paper demanding the reforms of Taobao. Although Alibaba agreed that the platform should be responsible for the governance of inauthentic goods, the group insisted that the regulator's law enforcement was "emotionally charged", and the procedure was illegal, therefore Alibaba filed a complaint against the SAIC department that was in charge of the investigation. Later, the SAIC announced officially that the white paper had no legal effect, and Alibaba withdrew the complaint. As an article reprinted by Xinhua News Agency stated, this incident is "the most heated confrontation between the government and an enterprise in the era of Internet economy" thus far.

However, five years later, the regulators initiated far more stringent actions against the Chinese online platforms. In November 2020, the Ant Financial Hong Kong IPO was halted by domestic regulators due to what they said was the potential systemic risk Ant might cause to the financial industry (Alison, 2020). Few people realized that the investigation against Ant Financial would initiate the promulgation of a series of regulations and investigation of the whole Internet industry, especially on the large online platforms. Since the end of 2020, the antitrust investigations, for a variety of reasons, were initiated against the platforms. These included illegal requirements that customers must maintain exclusive relationships with one or the other of the e-commerce platforms, a lack of labour protection in the operations of gig economy platforms, and lax data security on ride-hailing platforms. At the end, new regulations were promulgated regarding platform news-feed algorithms (Arjun & Cheng, 2021). In other words, the investigations were on a whole range of issues ranging from technologies to business models. Interestingly, the regulatory pressure was largely imposed exclusively on the online giants that had benefited most from the previously loose regulatory environments.

In the case of Tencent, three related fields came under regulatory pressure, each of which was one of its main revenue sources. In Table 7.1 the main sources of revenue and growth in 2020 for Tencent are presented. Games revenue is included in value-added service, taking 32% of the total.

Table 7.1 Tencent revenue sources and growth from 2019 to 2020

Business	*Per cent of Revenue*	*Growth (yoy)*
Value-Added Service	55%	32%
Online Ads	17%	20%
FinTech and Business Service	27%	26%
Other	1%	

Source: Tencent Annual Report 2020, https://static.www.tencent.com/uploads/2021/04/08/960eae1f18dd716fd3a7d704e123d7a5.pdf), accessed 07.10.2021

Fintech and mobile payments

As it was discussed in Jia and Kenney (2021), Tencent was most successful in strengthening its PBG model in mobile payments by embedding it in its super instant messaging apps, WeChat and QQ. Introduced in 2014Q2, WeChat Pay enjoyed the benefits of the existing user base of WeChat, while it strengthened WeChat's network effects in turn. Until 2017Q4, WeChat Pay had accounted for 38.15% of all domestic online payments trailing only Alipay which occupied 54.26%. Together, they control the overwhelming share of the online payment market. Based on payment service and the transaction data accumulated from the users, Tencent developed the credit-rating scheme that allowed it to expand to other financial services like providing micro-loans and selling mutual funds, thereby competing with the Alipay–Ant Financial services.

Most of these platform firms had experienced very little regulation – in fact, the government was very supportive of their growth (McKnight et al., 2021). One of the few enforcements was between 2015 and 2019, when Tencent was investigated by the Central Bank and State Administration of Foreign Exchange for violating the financial regulations. However, the penalty of less than 1 million RMB was minimal. At this time, Tencent was judged to be a neutral intermediary and not a financial institution. However, in 2021, similar to Alibaba, the government's view changed, and Tencent was required to separate financial services from the payment service (Zhang et al., 2021). The payment systems were not considered to be financial institutions that should be put under the much tighter financial market regulations. Regardless of penalties, the modification of the regulatory oversight of its business model had a far more serious impact on Tencent's revenues and ability to make decisions.

Gaming industry

The global gaming industry grew rapidly during the pandemic. Tencent's gaming business is an iconic example of the PBG model (Coe & Yang, 2021). However, the Chinese gaming platforms now confront far more regulatory scrutiny in their very lucrative domestic market. In 2021, the Ministry of Education initiated a nationwide reform aimed at developing what it believes is a healthier and more active environment for students. One of the most surprising new policies was to ban the after-school tutoring industry. This was implemented to limit the pressure on students to constantly prepare themselves for examinations, thereby providing more time for exercise. The result of these sweeping new rules was that the entire, largely online, private education industry business model, the largest firms of which had been listed on US markets, was put at the risk of becoming defunct.

The reforms were not limited to education. The gaming industry was affected when the National Press and Publication Administration (NPPA) issued a policy requiring that minors under 18 be blocked from playing video games for more than three hours a week with a maximum of one hour a day. Although Tencent declared that minors were not a significant source of revenue, as they made up only 2.6% of its total in 2021Q2, the investors still expected a negative impact on the future growth of the gaming industry.

Still other regulatory challenges to the gaming industry came from antitrust investigations. For example, Huya and Douyu, the two largest live game-streaming firms in China and listed on the US market, had planned to merge, but the merger was vetoed in July 2021 by the State Administration for Market Regulation (SAMR). This affected Tencent because it is the largest shareholder of Huya and holds more than one-third of the shares of Douyu. This merger was in keeping with the previously accepted PBG model. This contrasted with 2015, when four large mergers between DiDi and Kuaidi, Meituan and Dianping, 58 and Ganji, and Ctrip and Qunar, all leading companies in an industrial vertical, were approved with no questions asked.

Social networks

The social network industry of Tencent is built around two super apps, WeChat and QQ. In contrast to western counterparts that are focused on vertical markets, Tencent leveraged its social network platform to expand horizontally to other industries, thereby strengthening its PBG model. In previous years, Tencent had invested in travel (Tongcheng-Yilong), ride hailing (DiDi), e-commerce (JD, VIP Shop, Pingduoduo), local delivery services (58.com, Meituan-Dianping), a search engine (Sogou), telecommunications (China Unicom), a short video platform (Kuaishou), an online car retailer (Guazi, Renrenche), live broadcasting (Huya, Douyu), news (Qutoutiao), and other services. Receiving Tencent's investments gave firms the ability to secure traffic driven by Tencent's services such as WeChat. These alliances increased data sharing and through analysis of the data could allow a more complete picture of users to target advertising. For example, almost immediately after the Tencent-JD cross-investment in 2017, the two firms announced the launch of the JD-Tencent Retail Marketing Solution that was meant to integrate "insights on consumer behaviour from Tencent's social platforms with online and offline shopping data from JD and its brand partners." With this they claimed to have developed "the industry's most comprehensive toolkit for understanding consumer shopping behaviours and enable more precise target marketing and greater impact for brands".

The PBG model that was central to Tencent's business model is now receiving regulatory scrutiny. The current concerns for regulators are data security risks and the anti-competitive practices. In 2021, two important laws, Data Security Law and Personal Information Protection Act, were passed establishing a comprehensive and strict regulatory environment concerning the individual data rights and collective data security. However, these directly affected the existing business model practices of the platform firms as their current practices likely do not comply with the new rules. For example the Ministry of Industry and Information Technology (MIIT) announced that WeChat illegally utilized the users' contacts information and location data for commercial purposes and demanded modifications of the super applications in August 2021 (Feng & Chan, 2021).

This is difficult because the PBG strategy depends upon the super apps channelling traffic to other services that Tencent invests in. Further, Tencent had closed its ecosystem to competitors thus forming a "walled garden" that excludes competitors, but this is violating the new competition laws. In September 2021, the MIIT demanded that online platforms should stop blocking competitors' links and to open those links to each other's instant messaging platforms in an effort to create a fair and open competitive environment. As a result, WeChat and QQ had to drop their traditional practices that blocked external links from apps like Taobao or TikTok.

The result of all of these Chinese regulatory changes has been that the PBG model is now being forced to evolve in new directions. In the next section, the question of how this might change their strategies regarding overseas markets will be explored.

Tencent's global expansion strategy shift

Once it was argued that despite the extremely rich ecosystems within the protected Chinese market, the PBG model that Chinese online giants formed would be difficult to transfer to global markets (Jia and Kenney, 2021). At the time, we argued that there was little evidence that they posed a significant threat to West Coast platform firms outside of the gaming industry. One of the important reasons is that the regulatory environment in global markets would be less likely to accept the horizontal expansions and acquisitions that allowed the creation of the PBG model. Of course, the relatively large domestic market in China also weakened the motivations of online platform firms to expand internationally where they normally had to compete with West Coast incumbents. For example, in late 2000s, Baidu once had ambitions to expand its search engine service globally. After experiencing limited success, Baidu withdrew from most of their overseas businesses and refocused on the domestic market. Even for Tencent, despite enormous investments on the globalization of WeChat, the super app still was unable to challenge the incumbents like the Japanese messaging app, LINE, and the US messaging app, WhatsApp.

However, as domestic regulatory pressure increases, it has become difficult for Chinese platform giants to continue benefiting from the domestic institutional voids that helped establish the PBG model. As a result, these firms have been forced to invest overseas to compete with local incumbents instead of staying in the domestic market. The accelerated global investments of Tencent in 2021 illustrate this response to the domestic regulatory changes.

Tencent's overseas investments have increased in 2021 (see Table 7.2). This is particularly evident when comparing 2016 to 2020 investments to those in

Table 7.2 Total sum of Tencent's investments (2016H–2020H)

Year	*2016H*	*2017H*	*2018H*	*2019H*	*2020H*	*2021H*
Sum/Billion RMB	80	146	354	417	540	844

Source: Financial reports of Tencent 2016–2020.

mid-2020 and mid-2021, after the change in the Chinese regulatory regime. In the first half of 2021, Tencent made 163 investments with a total sum of 93.1 billion RMB domestically and globally. In contrast, in the first half of 2020, Tencent only made 60 investments. Moreover, Tencent's investments were concentrated in games and business services. In the first half of 2021, Tencent had 50 investments in the gaming industry and 33 in business services. Many of these investments were in the domestic market; however, it is the overseas investments that were more salient, both for Tencent and the understanding of the future expansion strategy of Chinese platform firms. Gaming and business services are critical for Tencent's overseas expansion strategy shift. Further, due to the US–China trade conflicts, Tencent has halted investing in US companies and shifted towards Europe.

A Shift to PC and console games in Europe

With the deepening rift between the United States and China and the implementation of new regulatory regime in China, Tencent's investment geography has changed significantly. To illustrate, in the first half of 2021, of the 12 overseas gaming investments by Tencent, 7 were in Europe (see Table 7.3).

Coe and Yang (2021) showed that Tencent used mobile gaming production to increase their market power (Coe & Yang, 2021). Tencent had concentrated its investments in the mobile gaming industry, including some of its most important transactions like Supercell and Riot Games. It also invested in Epic Games, which is a multi-platform gaming firm. In 2021, Tencent appears to have pivoted to PC and console games.

There were two important reasons for Tencent initially emphasizing mobile games. First, Chinese access to the Internet was overwhelmingly through mobile devices. Second, as a large PBG, Tencent had an organizational advantage by which it could utilize its powerful mobile distribution network to advertise and even persuade Chinese users to play mobile games. In other words, Tencent's

Table 7.3 Investments in gaming industry of Tencent in Europe

Name	*Country*	*Industry*
Sumo Group	UK	PC, Console, and Mobile Game Developer and Distributor Support
Dontnod Entertainment	France	PC and Console Game Developer
Bohemia Interactive	Czech Republic	PC Game Developer
Yager	Germany	PC Game Developer
Stunlock Studio	Sweden	PC Game Developer
Fatsshark	Sweden	PC and Console Game Developer and Distributer
Remedy Entertainment	Finland	PC Game Developer

Source: Based on author's collected online news and the companies' official websites.

foreign investments were in mobile games that it could then introduce to domestic consumers. This can be seen by the fact that in 2020, only 21% of Tencent's total games' revenue was from outside China (Niko, 2021). Prior to the government crackdown, which recently extended to government-mandated hourly limits of gameplay per week for young persons, the Chinese gaming market was extremely attractive.

The "import-games-into-China" strategy changed in 2021, as can be seen by the fact that all seven of its 2021 investments in Europe were in PC and console game developers. In the global markets, mobile game profits are limited because the Google Play Store and Apple AppStore receive 30% of all revenues generated by a game, therefore capturing a large share of total profits. In contrast, in China, the application store is controlled by Tencent.

As PC and console games are more popular outside of China and profits are higher, these investments indicate that Tencent aims to diversify its gaming revenue model by expanding beyond mobile games. Additionally, this shift might also be a shifting signature of Tencent to be a real global game producer and distributor serving global consumers rather than just importing games for domestic users.

Another change of the expansion strategy is the geographic transition from the United States to the EU. According to our database prior to 2020, of Tencent's 30 overseas investments in gaming industry, nearly 50% were in US firms, while less than 20% were in EU firms. The EU investments included firms such as Supercell, Miniclip SA, Zam, and Paradox Interactive. (Jia et al., 2018). It can be hypothesized that the trade war between China and the United States and the regulatory uncertainty in both countries have led Tencent to the EU as an ecosystem for investment.

The expansion of business services operations in Europe

While gaming industry has received the most investment from Tencent, it has also invested in business service firms, particularly in FinTech, and been establishing data centres. In the first quarter, 2021, total business service revenues were 39 billion RMB (US $6 billion) experiencing an annual growth rate of 47%. Further, business service revenues were 27% of its total revenue and increased to the second largest source of revenues. The most important source of the increase in revenues was the payment platform embedded in WeChat. Tencent used the relationships with its affiliates to embed the WeChat payment function into all of its activities and those of its PBG partners, thereby directing payment to itself.

Strategically, Tencent has wanted to export its business model globally. However, it has very little success. For this reason, Tencent has invested in overseas payment service providers hoping it could participate in their success in their home markets. For example, in 2020, Tencent led Lydia's $45 billion Series B funding round while Lydia's executives say frankly that the company wants to create a financial hub within the payment app to offer customers a suite of financial services, a strategy very much similar to WeChat payment.

Given its increasingly large global footprint, Tencent has been establishing data centres overseas. Data centres are the core of cloud computing, and for large firms establishing their own data centres it provides independence from depending on a data centre owned by a potential competitor such as Google, Amazon, Microsoft, etc. In June 2021, Tencent announced it had established four new data centres, three of which were in Asia (Bangkok, Thailand; Hong Kong; and Tokyo, Japan) and one in Europe (Frankfurt, Germany). As of 2021, Tencent operates in 68 of what it terms "availability zones" globally. In Europe, it operates five centres located in Moscow (one), London (one), Amsterdam (one), and Frankfurt (two).

The increase of overseas data centres suggests that Tencent is experiencing growing cloud service demand, much of which is driven by the gaming empire it has built. For example, prior to being acquired by Tencent, Supercell relied upon Amazon for cloud service, but it has since transitioned to the Tencent cloud. Further, some have suggested that in the future, all of Supercell's mobile games might be hosted by the Tencent cloud. Given the difficulty of challenging Amazon or Microsoft or even Google on enterprise compute customers, the online gaming industry is likely the way Tencent can gain traction in the global cloud service market.

Discussion and conclusion

Illustrated by the case of Tencent, we show that the changes in the domestic regulatory environment of China have driven the Chinese online giants to more actively explore the foreign market for growth. When the Chinese regulatory environment was supportive, the Chinese platform giants created the PBG model and exploited the rapidly growing domestic market. After the regulatory regime shifts, the PBG model itself has become a target of regulations, forcing them to accelerate the globalization strategy. However, this does not necessarily mean that the PBG will fail. More likely, it will evolve into a different configuration.

In 2021, Tencent's overseas investments accelerated. Moreover, the expansions appear to be different from those undertaken earlier. First, in the gaming industry, the expansion of Tencent from mobile games to PC and console games, whose investments were largely located in Europe, suggests the possible shift from merely satisfying domestic demands to serving international customers. Second, it is accelerating the building of data centres internationally, but, in particular, in Europe and Southeast Asia. By providing cloud-computing services to online games, Tencent could internalize its gaming industry traffic. It might even be possible to challenge the western cloud service incumbents, including Amazon and Microsoft. The equity investments in independent gaming firms that are then connected to Tencent cloud services are a typical strategy of the PBG model. This suggests a possible transitional form compared with the domestic model that is built on super apps and payment platforms. The next question would be whether Tencent could leverage payment provision or create a super app in foreign markets.

The United States has traditionally been the market that received the most investments by Tencent. However, given the deepening trade friction with the United States and regulatory uncertainty, Tencent's investment patterns have changed. Tencent has ceased investing in US firms, while increasing its investments in Europe. Despite some critics arguing that gaming industry investments should also be under review for data protection and national security concern, most of the transactions were not being examined (Haeck, 2021). It is possible that there will be future investigations of Chinese gaming acquisitions, if it turns out that the gaming investments are judged to violate individuals' data rights or somehow pose a national security risk.

Generalizing from a single case study with regards to the strategy impact of the emerging regulatory regime in China is risky, and our results are tentative. The changing regulatory environment appears to have created an impetus for the Chinese platform firms to look abroad for new markets, and Europe, with its strong gaming industry, has proven attractive for Tencent. Thus far, it appears as though in terms of gaming, the European governments have not considered these firms of sufficient national security, technical know-how, or systemic importance to consider blocking Chinese investment. The future evolution of Tencent's globalization strategy in Europe will, in part, be determined by the geopolitical conflict between China and the United States and the domestic regulatory developments.

8 Baltic trade with three major Asian economies

Structural breaks and macroeconomic determinants

Hegerty Scott

Introduction

The Baltic nations of Estonia, Latvia, and Lithuania are small open economies that do the vast majority of their international trade with their neighbours. Besides buying each other's goods and services, the Baltics export to and import from the Nordic region, Western and Central Europe, and Russia. At the same time, large Asian countries do so much trade that pure economic size overcomes the effects of distance. As a result, there is substantial trade between the Baltics and the economic powerhouses of China, Japan, and India. These bilateral relationships have yet to be studied in the economic literature in much detail.

While approaches such as the "gravity model" (which uses country GDP and distance as key determinants of trade flows) are often popular, macroeconomic analyses typically use some modification of the approach of Goldstein and Khan (1985). In this model, export and import flows are the functions of foreign and domestic income, respectively (and trade balances depend on both); price effects are captured by price levels, the terms of trade, or (commonly) the real exchange rate. A number of previous empirical studies have been reviewed by Bahmani-Oskooee and Ratha (2004), with a focus on the so-called "J-Curve" phenomenon; this literature has expanded greatly since.

In particular, the role of exchange-rate volatility, which might – but does not necessarily have to – reduce trade flows, has been incorporated into numerous empirical models. Early studies of this type include analyses by Chowdhury (1993) and Cushman (1992). As has been shown in reviews by McKenzie (1999) and Bahmani-Oskooee and Hegerty (2007), risk often has only a limited impact. This might be because of effective hedging by multinational corporations. Increased volatility might actually increase export or import flows if traders are sufficiently "risk-loving." As a result, the signs and significances of any volatility terms are highly idiosyncratic.

The Baltic countries have received little attention outside broader analyses of the Central and Eastern European (CEE) region. One study of interest, however, is by Moslares and Ekanayake (2018), who examine both aggregate and bilateral exports for all three countries and find that exchange-rate volatility indeed has mixed effects. China is included as a trade partner for Estonia and Latvia (with

DOI: 10.4324/9781003274933-8

very different results for each country); India and Japan are not included as any Baltic export partner.

A number of recent studies have focused specifically on Asian trade, using a variety of new and established methods. Upadhyaya et al. (2020) examine a panel of ASEAN-5 countries (Thailand, Malaysia, Singapore, the Philippines, and Indonesia), finding that income and terms of trade and volatility all have significant effects on export flows in various cases and that exchange-rate volatility reduces trade flows for the group as a whole.

For the case of Japan, Bahmani-Oskooee et al. (2017) apply asymmetric cointegration techniques to determine the separate effects of yen appreciations and depreciations on the country's trade balance. Jiang et al. (2020) use Vector Error Correction methods to focus on Japan's exports as a function of world income, imports, and the real exchange rate. Nonlinear, asymmetric methods are now commonly used for many countries, including in Asia; examples include Bahmani-Oskooee et al. (2018) for China and Bahmani-Oskooee and Saha (2017, 2021) for India.

While Hegerty (2020) uses similar methods in other contexts, the application of structural breaks in trade models has received comparatively less attention in the literature. Ketenci (2016) conducts a series of tests on the EU's quarterly export and import flows with a number of partners worldwide (including the three countries examined in the current study, as well as South Korea). After conducting a number of structural break tests, cointegration analysis is performed using income and price effects as controls. The authors confirm that structural breaks are an important component of trade modelling.

This study examines structural breaks for nine Baltic–Asian trade balances, identifying specific dates and the statistical properties of these flows between and within "regimes" or sub periods, before including these breaks for an estimation of the determinants of each trade balance. Overall, Estonia's trade has the fewest structural breaks, and Indian trade is driven most strongly by the traditional macroeconomic determinants.

This chapter proceeds as follows. Section 8.2 outlines the methodology. Section 8.3 discusses the results, and Section 8.4 concludes.

Methodology

Monthly data from the International Monetary Fund's Direction of Trade Statistics (DOTS) are used for the three Baltic countries' bilateral exports and imports vis-à-vis China, India, and Japan. Additional data for the U.S. Consumer Price Index (to deflate the nominal trade flow data, which are in dollars), as well as the nine countries' indices of industrial production, are sourced from the IMF's International Financial Statistics, and monthly measures of the three Asian Countries' real effective exchange rates (REERs) are taken from the Bank for International Settlements via the FRED database. Each time series is de-seasonalized using the Census-X12 procedure.

The nine real bilateral export and import series (for three Baltic countries and three partners) are presented in Figure 8.1. Trade with China, in particular, appears

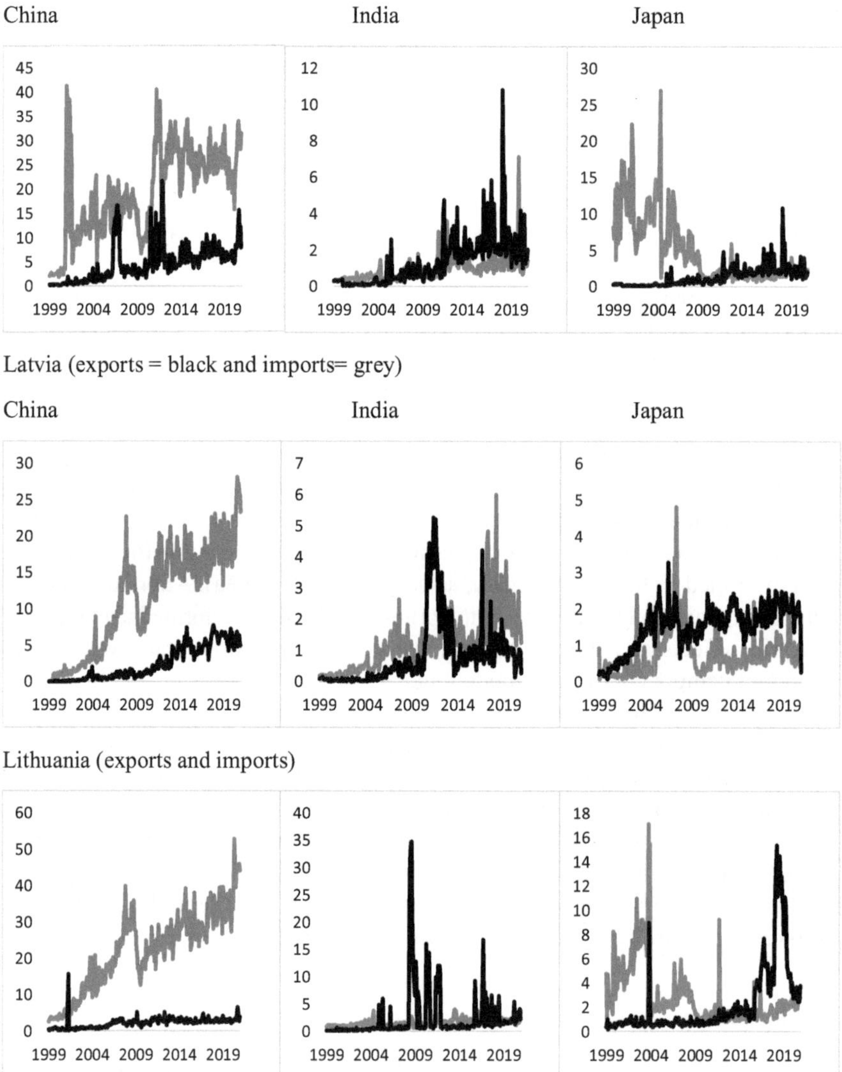

Figure 8.1 Bilateral trade flow series (millions of US dollars per month).

Source: Calculated by the author based on International Monetary Fund data.

to be growing during the period under investigation. Estonia registers a trade deficit throughout much of the sample, since imports exceed exports. Estonia's deficit vis-à-vis Japan, on the other hand, closes over time.

It is these dynamics that this study aims to address. To do so, each bilateral real trade balance (exports minus imports) is plotted over time. The Bai and Perron (1998) structural break test is then implemented to formally identify regime shifts in the data. R packages developed by Zeileis et al. (2002, 2003) are implemented for this procedure.

This method can use any underlying model; here, the focus is on the trade balances themselves, so this is equivalent to applying it to a regression on a constant. Once these regimes are isolated, the means and standard deviations of the trade balances within each subperiod are calculated and compared. The nonparametric Kruskal and Wallis (1952) test is used to test the significance of the differences in means across multiple sub periods. The structural breakpoints are also used in the subsequent cointegration analysis of the determinants of each trade balance.

These breakpoints are also included in a cointegration estimation of the determinants of each bilateral trade balance. Following the classic model of Goldstein and Khan (1985), the underlying macroeconomic variables include exporter and importer income, proxied by the monthly index of industrial production, with competitiveness measured by the Asian exporter's real effective exchange rate. In this model, REER volatility is included as a proxy for risk; as Bahmani-Oskooee and Hegerty (2007, 2009) note, while this might be expected to reduce trade, it might also increase it in some cases – or have no effect at all. REER volatility is calculated using a GARCH model (as in Bollerslev, 1986), using a traditional Autoregressive Moving Average (ARMA) process, chosen via the Box–Jenkins method. GARCH-based measures are compared against a simpler measure calculated as 12-month moving standard deviations of each REER series and are found to be quite similar.

The model to be estimated can therefore be written as:

$$TB_t = f\left(Y_t^H, Y_t^F, REER_t, REERVOL_t\right) \tag{1}$$

Following Bahmani-Oskooee and Hegerty (2009), this model is estimated using the Autoregressive Distributive Lag (ARDL) approach of Pesaran et al. (2001). While the focus of the current study is on the long-run estimates, this method also produces short-run estimators within a single equation. More importantly, the ARDL approach allows for the inclusion of both stationary and nonstationary variables without differentiating. The presence of a long-run cointegrating relationship is established via an F-test for the joint significance of the long-run variables in the ARDL equation.

While newer methods, such as the Nonlinear ARDL method of Shin et al. (2014), are used to capture asymmetries in the responses to positive and negative shocks, here the standard linear approach is used. It will show the relative influence of income and price effects, as well as risk, across the Baltics as well as vis-à-vis different Asian trade partners. Overall, significant variation in effects is shown. The results are provided later in the chapter.

Results

Figure 8.2 depicts all nine trade balances (for three Baltic countries and three Asian partners) over the sample period. In addition, structural breakpoints,

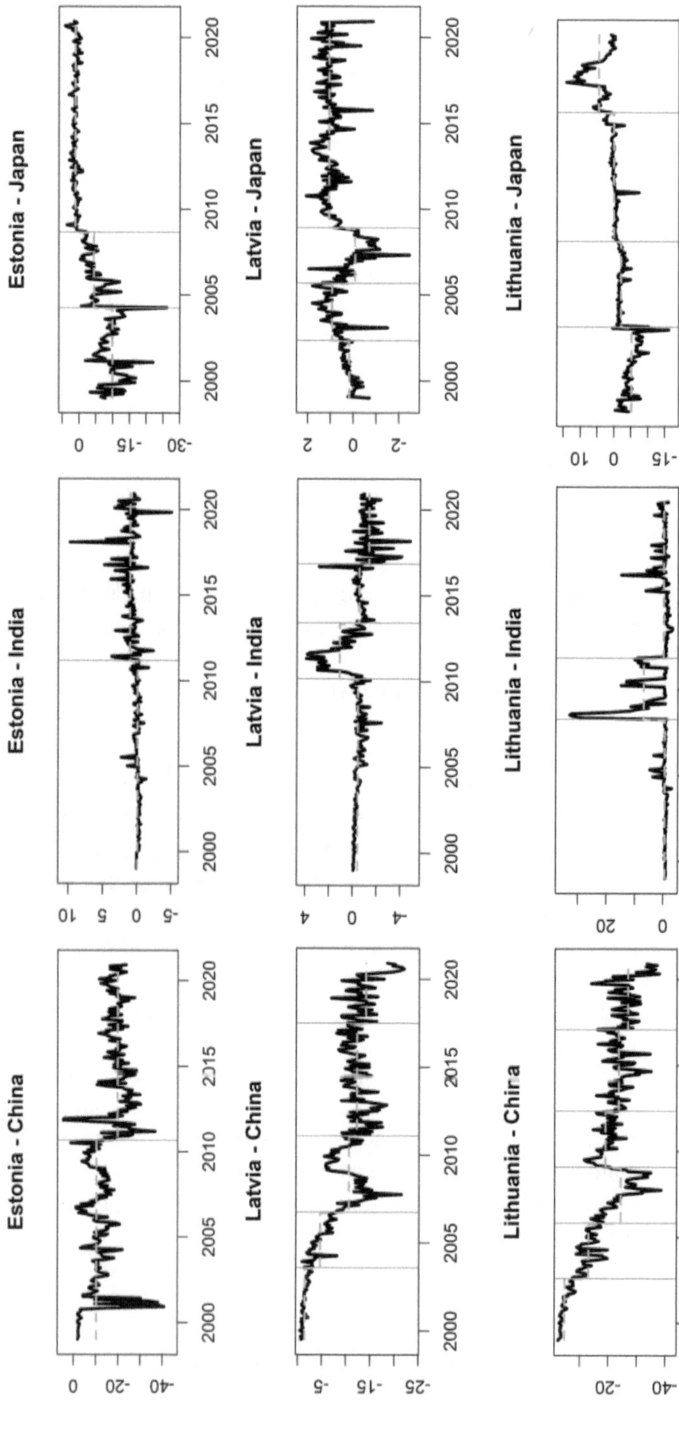

Figure 8.2 Bilateral trade balances and structural breaks.

Vertical lines: structural breaks. Horizontal lines: sub-period means.

Source: Author's calculations.

obtained via the Bai and Perron (1998) test, divide the sample (vertically), and the within-period means are shown (horizontally). Specific dates for breakpoints, as well as precise means and standard deviations, are also given in Table 8.1. Latvia's trade balance with China, for example, goes from near-balance to a mild deficit early on, with deterioration following September 2006. This is likely due to the "overheating" and capital-flow "bonanza" during this period, which combined with a fixed exchange rate lead to a pre-crisis economic boom. The deficit stabilized beginning in 2011; however. Estonia's trade deficit with Japan, on the other hand, closed following the 2008 crisis. Lithuania's trade balance with Japan crept from a deficit to balanced trade to a surplus, but other pairs (such as with India) remain relatively flat. Overall, Estonia has the fewest structural breaks across all partners (4, compared to 10 for Latvia and Lithuania). The Kruskal and Wallis (1952) test shows the means to be significantly different across subperiods in all cases. Further research would be necessary to investigate the direct causes of each change in trade regime.

These results are interesting overall because they can be used in further research to identify specific events and causes of each structural change. These breaks are also entered into the cointegration model as given later in the chapter. One key variable is exchange-rate risk, which has the potential to reduce export and/or

Table 8.1 Structural breaks and associated statistics

Pair	*Breaks: Year(Month)*	*Regime #: Mean (SD)*					*Kruskall–Wallis*
		1	*2*	*3*	*4*	*6*	*Stat (p-val)*
EE-CH	2010(8)	−10.22 (7.02)	−19.65 (5.69)				123.8 (0.00)
EE-IN	2011(2)	−0.10 (0.43)	1.05 (1.48)				112.6 (0.00)
EE-JP	2004(3), 2008(8)	−9.94 (4.18)	−4.43 (4.06)	1.14 (0.87)			202.9 (0.00)
LV-CH	2003(7), 2006(9), 2011(1), 2017(6)	−1.46 (0.59)	−4.68 (2.04)	−10.6 (3.35)	−12.24 (2.51)	−14.08 (3.70)	183.9 (0.00)
LV-IN	2010(2), 2013(5), 2016(10)	−0.44 (0.37)	1.08 (1.51)	−0.54 (0.65)	−1.36 (1.04)		96.9 (0.00)
LV-JP	2002(4), 2005(8), 2008(11)	0.18 (0.29)	0.93 (0.56)	−0.08 (0.78)	1.07 (0.45)		125.8 (0.00)
LT-CH	2002(7), 2005(10), 2009(1), 2012(4), 2017(1)	−4.74 (1.76)	−13.05 (3.33)	−24.32 (6.12)	−19.02 (3.36)	−23.65 (3.89)	190.0 (0.00)
LT-IN	2008(3), 2011(10)	−0.58 (0.93)	6.89 (9.39)	−0.07 (2.34)			39.9 (0.00)
LT-JP	2003(11), 2008(11), 2016(5)	−5.22 (2.73)	−2.09 (1.39)	0.06 (1.22)	4.55 (3.81)		216.1 (0.00)

Source: Author's calculations.

Table 8.2 GARCH estimates for REER volatility.

	China	*India*	*Japan*
mu	0.106 (0.294)	0.048 (0.616)	−0.123 (0.461)
ar1	0.315 (0.000)	0.092 (0.124)	0.245 (0.000)
ar2	−0.065 (0.275)		
omega	0.059 (0.536)	0.081 (0.309)	0.272 (0.276)
alpha1	0.037 (0.265)	0.029 (0.159)	0.062 (0.056)
beta1	0.926 (0.000)	0.936 (0.000)	0.883 (0.000)

P-values in parentheses.

import flows. To measure this, monthly log changes in the real effective exchange rates are modelled using an ARMA (p, q) process with GARCH (1,1) errors. The three countries are shown to follow an AR (1) or AR (2) process, as shown by the following equation:

$$\Delta lnREER_t = \mu + \rho_1 \Delta lnREER_{t-1} + \rho_2 \Delta lnREER_{t-2} + \varepsilon_t \quad (2a)$$

$$h_t = \omega + \alpha_1 \varepsilon^2 + \beta_1 h_{t-1} \quad (2b)$$

Table 8.2 provides the results. The estimated variance series – real exchange-rate risk – are shown in Figure 8.3. They behave similarly – but not identically – to risk measures calculated as rolling standard deviations. As might be expected, volatility is highest following the 1998 Asian Crisis and the 2008 Global Financial Crisis.

The final objective of this study is to estimate the determinants of each trade balance using the macroeconomic relationships depicted in Equation (1). This is done via the ARDL method of Pesaran et al. (2001) as is noted before, and this model works with both stationary variables that are I(0), or nonstationary variables that are integrated of order one. Table 8.3 shows that the trade balances examined here are stationary in levels, based on the Phillips and Perron (1988) test.

It is assumed that income would be nonstationary, but this is not shown via this test. Both I (0) and I (1) variables can be found in thus dataset. Regardless of the specific orders of integration, the ARDL approach is a good choice given the potential mix of I (0) and I (1) variables.

The results of the ARDL model, which is estimated using the "ARDL" package in R with the variable lags chosen by minimizing the Akaike Information Criterion, are presented in Table 8.4 of the key macroeconomic determinants of these trade balances; risk only reduces the trade balance in one instance (between Estonia and China). Japan's connections are weakest; no variables are significant, and the F-statistics supporting cointegration is low. Indian income has a significant impact on trade with Estonia and Lithuania, and the weakening rupee REER boosts the trade balances of Latvia and Lithuania. Stronger Latvian income leads to a trade deficit with China, likely through increased imports; Lithuania's coefficients, on the other hand, have signs that are opposite from what might

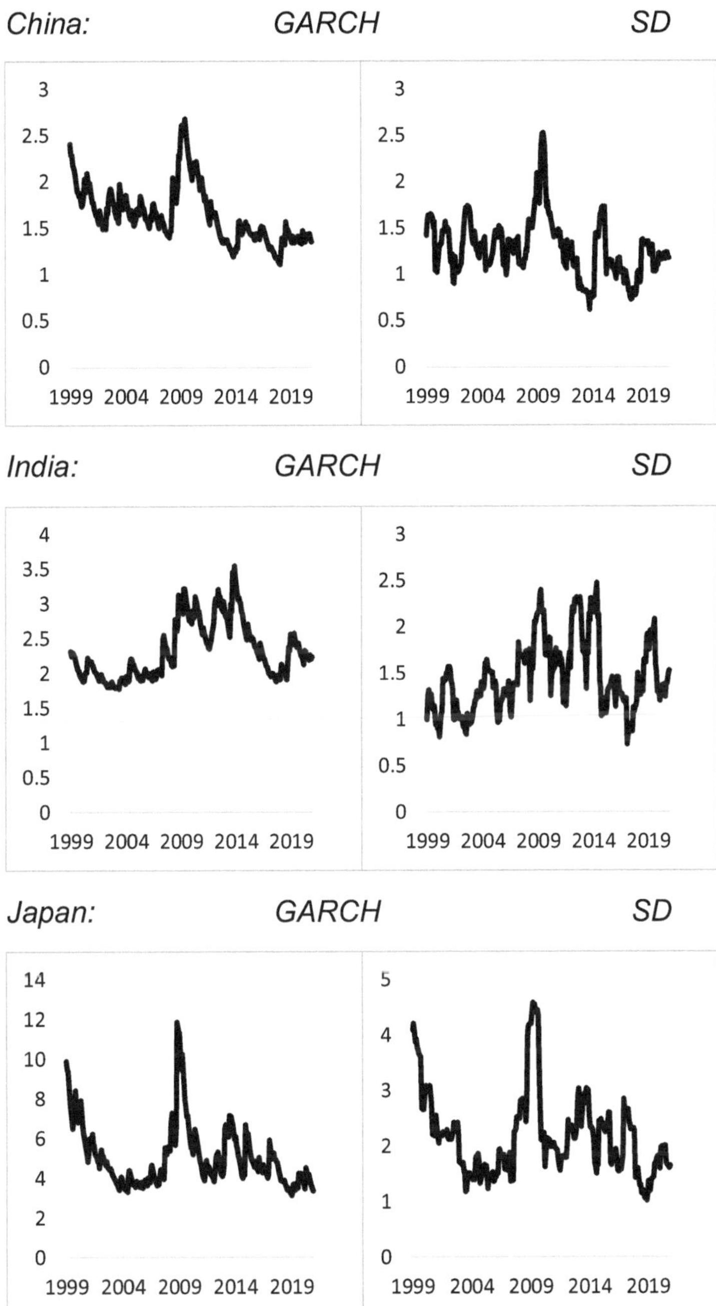

Figure 8.3 Measures of REER volatility.

Source: Calculated by the author based on Bank for International Settlements data.

Table 8.3 Phillips–Perron stationarity test results.

Trade Balances	*Levels*	*First Diff.*
EE-CH	−8.565 (0.01)	−26.279 (0.01)
EE-IN	−14.931 (0.01)	−41.541 (0.01)
EE-JP	−8.879 (0.01)	−33.616 (0.01)
LV-CH	−6.459 (0.01)	−31.223 (0.01)
LV-IN	−7.705 (0.01)	−34.122 (0.01)
LV-JP	−8.744 (0.01)	−36.129 (0.01)
LT-CH	−6.044 (0.01)	−26.965 (0.01)
LT-IN	−5.801 (0.01)	−18.610 (0.01)
LT-JP	−6.910 (0.01)	−34.472 (0.01)
Macro Variables	*Levels*	*First Diff.*
China REER	−2.009 (0.57)	−11.591 (0.01)
India REER	−3.296 (0.07)	−14.322 (0.01)
Japan REER	−2.532 (0.35)	−12.273 (0.01)
China REERVOL	−3.64 (0.03)	−14.861 (0.01)
India REERVOL	−3.643 (0.03)	−18.763 (0.01)
Japan REERVOL	−3.16 (0.10)	−13.925 (0.01)
Estonia IP	−6.41 (0.01)	−31.316 (0.01)
Latvia IP	−6.279 (0.01)	−21.483 (0.01)
Lithuania IP	−6.903 (0.01)	−27.442 (0.01)
China IP	−6.792 (0.01)	−34.126 (0.01)
India IP	−7.539 (0.01)	−28.374 (0.01)
Japan IP	−3.162 (0.09)	−13.754 (0.01)

Source: Author's calculations.

Table 8.4 ARDL cointegration test results.

Estonia	*China*	*India*	*Japan*
IP_F	−0.406 (0.208)	**0.015 (0.049)**	0.075 (0.525)
IP_H	0.047 (0.268)	−0.001 (0.846)	−0.023 (0.598)
REER	−0.122 (0.371)	−0.006 (0.765)	−0.066 (0.175)
REERVOL	**5.072 (0.041)**	−0.322 (0.089)	0.107 (0.779)
Adj. R^2	0.91	0.34	0.84
F	9.83 (0.000)	6.02 (0.001)	6.60 (0.001)
ARDL Order	(8,12,1,2,0)	(9,6,0,0,0)	(5,12,0,5,1)

Latvia	*China*	*India*	*Japan*
IP_F	0.049 (0.889)	−0.002 (0.851)	−0.036 (0.310)
IP_H	**−0.417 (0.000)**	**−0.032 (0.004)**	0.015 (0.372)
REER	0.204 (0.157)	**0.131 (0.001)**	0.018 (0.225)
REERVOL	−3.28 (0.234)	−0.229 (0.487)	0.171 (0.276)
Adj. R^2	0.97	0.66	0.82
F	3.73 (0.034)	7.55 (0.000)	3.47 (0.05)
ARDL Order	(11,3,7,8,3)	(7,0,3,9,0)	(10,10,5,5,3)
Lithuania	*China*	*India*	*Japan*
IP_F	−0.343 (0.663)	**−0.373 (0.000)**	0.173 (0.303)
IP_H	−0.078 (0.631)	**0.175 (0.000)**	−0.049 (0.596)
REER	−0.014 (0.959)	**0.244 (0.000)**	−0.003 (0.970)
REERVOL	2.408 (0.749)	−0.135 (0.906)	0.117 (0.806)
Adj. R^2	0.98	0.70	0.84
F	1.87 (0.414)	23.58 (0.000)	3.67 (0.037)
ARDL Order	(11,12,4,3,9)	(4,12,1,2,3)	(2,12,1,2,0)

Source: Author's calculations.

be expected. Increased "foreign" (Indian) income should increase Lithuania's exports, while domestic income should increase imports.

These findings, therefore, suggest that the Baltics' trade with India is most accurately tied to this model; perhaps alternative or extended research approaches would help resolve these ambiguities. In particular, the application of gravity models, the inclusion of asymmetries, or the addition of other variables to the baseline model would be beneficial in a future study.

Conclusion

The small open economies of Estonia, Latvia, and Lithuania are major European traders – but still conduct substantial trade with large exporters in Asia. These trade flows, however, have received scant attention in the literature. Understanding their time-series behaviour, as well as their macroeconomic determinants, is essential, particularly as China's economic influence in the world increases. This study analyses the monthly trade balances of each Baltic country vis-à-vis China, India, and Japan from 1999 to 2020. Structural break tests help isolate clear "regimes," whereby deficits become surpluses or vice-versa, for example. The means are significantly different across regimes in all nine cases, supporting the idea of clear structural changes in these trade flows. The breaks are also included in a cointegration estimation of the macroeconomic determinants of each trade balance. Domestic and foreign industrial production, as well as the real effective exchange rate, is among these determinants. Also included is a measure of risk, proxy as a GARCH (1,1) variance series from an ARMA model of log changes in each Asian REER. The ARDL approach of Pesaran et al. (2001) produces both a cointegration test and a set of long-run coefficient estimates and also allows for a mix of stationary and I(1) variables in the model. Overall, Estonia trade registers the fewest structural breaks for all partners, suggesting that the underlying economic processes are the most stable. Latvian and Lithuanian trade with China, on the other hand, shows the largest number of structural breaks (with the latter generating five Further research is necessary to determine the exact causes of these breaks, and particularly in which country each originated.

The ARDL cointegration results show highly idiosyncratic results among the nine trade balances examined here. Of the three Asian countries, India follows the "traditional" macroeconomic model most closely, in terms of both high F-statistics supporting cointegration and significant long-run coefficients. Exchange-rate risk has little effect overall, increasing Estonia's trade balance with China (perhaps though reducing imports). Income and price effects have relatively little effect, particularly for Lithuanian trade and trade with Japan.

These findings – particularly the structural breaks estimated here – might be useful for policymakers. Understanding past regime changes might be interesting from a historical perspective, or might be beneficial in crafting policies designed to achieve similar results. Similar studies could be conducted for other CEE countries or for economies elsewhere in the world.

Further research could expand beyond the limitations of the present study. As noted before, analyses of the asymmetric effects of macroeconomic variables have become quite popular in the literature in recent years. Such a study could distinguish between increased and decreased risk, for example, or could treat appreciations and depreciations (or growth and recessions) separately. Such analyses could help policymakers understand the main drivers of these very unique trade flows.

9 Foreign direct investment outflow from Asian countries

Impact on the EU economy

Robert Dygas and Artur Tomeczek

Introduction

The Foreign Direct Investment Outflow (FDIO) is a stream of capital outflow from one country (home country) to another one (host country) with the aim to control such investment. It is quite often related to the activity of multinational firms (MNCs) and also governments. Each country shapes its FDI politics to boost GDP growth and country wealth. FDIs are also related to Free Trade Agreements (FTAs) which are parts of them influencing foreign trade development. Since 2016, FDI is in a declining trend reaching a drop of 13% globally and is directed mainly to developing economies in Asia and Oceania. The largest FDIO countries in Asia were Japan and China in 2018 (UNCTAD, 2019). COVID-19 and global isolation which break existing Global Value Chains (GVCs) will strengthen the FDI downward trend by further 30–40% and also MNEs earnings in developed countries in EU-28 by 30% in 2020–2021 according to UNCTAD statement in March 2020 (UNCTAD, 2020a), but, in fact, it is difficult to project it as of today. Besides the impact of pandemic COVID-19, Brexit also put the EU in the position of the shrinkage of its budget by 12% and the European Council's introduction of a framework for screening FDIs in all member states in 2019 will also limit FDI inflow to EU nations. During 2010–2018, the EU was the main destination for FDIs reaching 6,295 billion EUR in 2017 with the creation of 16 million direct jobs (EU, 2019). Before coronavirus COVID-19, global trade between Asia and Europe was more promising especially from the perspective of partnership and free trade agreements as well. Free trade agreements between developing countries can facilitate regional cooperation, but trade treaties between developed and developing economies can lead to conflicts between producers and customers (Mukhopadhyay & Thomassin, 2010). Some of the important agreements are EU–South Korea Free Trade Agreement in 2011, EU–Japan Economic Partnership Agreement in 2019, and EU–India Strategic Partnership Agreement under changes since 2004. The FTA with South Korea generated 4.4 billion EUR in growth in EU Gross Domestic Product (GDP) during the first five years of its implementation. It also contributed to the protection of intellectual property rights, in particular, the enforcement and protection of EU geographical indications (EC, 2019). Concerning Japan, a special platform for

DOI: 10.4324/9781003274933-9

SME business exchange between Japan and EU and also EU–Japan Centre for Industrial Cooperation were established. In 2018, the EU released a new strategy on India and also strengthened its position with the Association of Southeast Asian Nations (ASEAN). The main aim of the strategic partnership of the EU with India is to mutually grow in economic and military perspectives securing the development of bilateral trade and investments by implementing Agenda 2030 (EU, 2018). India had a plan before COVID-19 to become a 6.9 trillion EUR economy by 2030 by establishing itself as a global hub for manufacturing, research, and innovation. The EU recognized this opportunity and has set up strategically targeted policy dialogues with India to increase business collaborations, trade, and investments (EEAS, 2018). In February 2019, Business Support to EU–India Policy Dialogues was established as a project governed by GFA Consulting Group GmbH (Hamburg, Germany) in consortium with EBTC – European Business and Technology Centre (New Delhi, India), implementation partner India and EUROCHAMBERS (Brussels, Belgium), and implementation partner Europe. Besides these important trade framework agreements with South Korea, Japan, and India, the EU also looked at the perspective of potential investment cooperation with other Asian countries like Vietnam, Malaysia, Thailand, and also EU-ASEAN Business Council (EU-ABC) was established in 2014 not only to facilitate trade and investment between Europe and ASEAN. Since 1975, the main and the most important country in Asia for the EU was China, and in 2003 Comprehensive Strategic Partnership Agreement was deepened and later on EU–China 2020 Strategic Agenda for Cooperation was proposed by the EC to enhance cooperation for win-win results. One of the key aspects was to develop investment of both sides by securing long-term access to EU and Chinese markets respectively and providing for strong protection to investors and their investments (EEAS, 2013). China was a strong competitor to ASEAN regarding FDI flows in 2010–2018. ASEAN region is expected rather to be more FDI inflow-oriented but due to the US–China trade war, COVID-19, and new economy after that, growing trade protectionism, multilateralism, and FDI screening policy across EU's member states countries make the future unpredictable. Besides that, globalization of the trade economy process creates multinational companies which are very strongly related to FDI activities and impacts the GDP growth of the host countries as well. Europe definitely needs closer tights with Asia to grow and develop. Since 1996, there is a special connectivity platform called Asian-Europe Meeting (ASEM) for dialogue and cooperation between Europe and Asia including ASEAN members. Thanks to this platform, the relations between Europe and Asia can be discussed and analysed on different levels using a dedicated framework with indicators related also to FDI (Becker et al., 2019). There are some other very recent initiatives dedicated to the EU and chosen Asian countries like India. The business as the example Support to the EU–India Policy Dialogues was raised in February 2018. This project is led by GFA Consulting Group GmbH (Hamburg, Germany) in consortium with EBTC – European Business and Technology Centre (New Delhi, India), implementation partner India and EUROCHAMBRES (Brussels, Belgium), and implementation partner Europe. All of these aforementioned examples confirm that Asia is a strategic investment option for Europe, and especially India can be a counterparty to China after the economic shock caused by COVID-19. This chapter starts with the overview of existing studies regarding FDIO from Asian countries to analyse the impact of FDIO on the EU-28 in the period 2010–2018 and finally makes some projections regarding the future of Asian FDIO to EU-27 (after Brexit). The logic of the chapter is to give an overview of how the FDI outflow from Asian countries impacts EU economic growth. The results are presented in Sections 9.4 and 9.5 of this chapter.

Literature review on FDI outflow from Asian countries, especially India, to the EU member states

Morris and Palakh (2016) analyse the relationship between outward foreign direct investment (OFDI) stocks pertaining to 34 OECD source and 160 destination countries (i.e. bilateral stocks) and other variables like the size of the economy, distance, and language on such cross country flows. The study used the gravity model as the research design. The study is a cross-country study and does not specifically focus on the outward FDI (OFDI) from India to other countries. Moris et al. analyse the underlying economics and policies and their impact on outward FDI from India. The study focused mainly on the outward FDI policy framework and its impact on the OFDI from India. It did not comprehensively cover the determinants of the OFDI from India. Kaushal (2018) uses Dunning's OLI framework to identify the country-specific macro-economic growth drivers encouraging OFDI from India. It does not capture OFDI status and determinants from India to the EU. Bitzer and Görg (2005) analyse the impact of inward as well as outward FDI on industry performance by using the Cobb–Douglas production function. The study covers 17 OECD countries and does not specifically focus on OFDI from India to the EU. Lipsey (2002) discusses the fear of an increase in unemployment in the home country while discussing the impact of OFDI in the home country. The chapter suggests that same is not confirmed by evidence. Further, the host countries experience an increase in wages of even the domestic form in the industries receiving FDI as the foreign firms often pay higher wages in comparison to local firms thereby changing the landscape. Foreign firms also generally exhibit higher productivity in comparison to the local firms. FDI also positively impacts the exports from the host country. According to the study, the spill-over impact of technology transfer is not very clear. Pradhan and Neelam (2008) analyse the OFDI from India by diving them into two phases; the first one from 1975 to 1991 and the other from 1991 onwards. Observation made is that OFDI from India considerably increased after 1991 and was across industries, unlike the first phase where it was concentrated to manufacturing. The intent of OGDI mainly has been market seeking, creation of strategic assets, connecting with specialized skills, and enhancing global competitiveness. Tolentino (2008) examines the relationship between home country-specific macroeconomic factors and the level of outward FDI of China and India through the use of time series analysis from 1982 to 2006. The study uses a vector autoregressive model and highlights that in the case of China, the per capita income, openness of the economy to international trade, interest rates, human capital, technological capability, exchange rate and its volatility, etc., do not impact OGDI from China. While, in the case of India, the national technological capability of India in certain industries leads to more OFDI from those industries. Ramachandran et al. (2004) suggests that there has been a change in the nature and scale of overseas engagement of Indian companies. Overseas capabilities of Indian firms are dependent on the competitive advantage of firms rather than the national endowments. Outsourcing, internationalisation, and multinationalization are three strategies that Indian firms have opted for while deciding on overseas operations. The literature regarding FDI outflow and specific aspects related to host economies is quite substantial, but still there is a gap in the analysis to see how such FDIO from Asian countries especially India impacts EU economic growth and if it is substantial or not.

Methodology

This chapter uses existing accessible data and information regarding the subject of study. As of today, more researches are conducted regarding FDIO from Asian countries to host economies, but still, a few are done regarding Indian FDIO on EU member states. A recent publication in 2021 of Prana Krishna Biswas and Robert Dygas gives such an overview (Biswas & Dygas, 2021). Even though some specific studies have been conducted to understand the determinants and the drivers of outward FDI from Asian countries to European ones, there are still gaps to understand such impact on CEE countries, especially Visegrad Group (V4) and Three Seas Initiative (3SI). Hence, there is scope for research to understand FDI outflow from Asian countries to EU Nations.

Data presented by World Bank, FDI, and UNCTAD reports are the main recent data that helped to build up the conclusions and projections for this subject. There is a lack of specific econometric or statistical models (e.g. multidimensional panel data analysis) showing the big picture of the current situation with FDI outflow from Asian countries to EU member states, and details of the main determinants of those flows can be hardly found. Additionally, it is quite difficult to evaluate such existing analysis due to a problem of data correctness and their reference to reality and the need for multidimensional perspectives including politics and geoeconomics. One good example would be the choice of the country from the perspective of Asian countries to invest in, where the possible values might be European. Analysis in such instances requires the use of multinomial logit/probit models. Depending upon data availability and the problem in question, there can be a natural requirement to use conditional logit models as well which are common in geography economics to estimating location choices (Herger & McCorriston, 2013).

The logistic model (or logit/probit model) is used to model the probability of a certain class or event existing such as pass/fail. This can be extended to model several classes of events, such as determining the probability of the FDI decision by Asian companies, the value of each determinant for FDI outflow, and the establishment of sister companies in the host countries. That kind of model is not enough to show the current situation globally with FDI outflow from Asian countries to EU nations. That is why this chapter is based on the available data and reports and why we try to expand upon them using network analysis.

Preparing the right model to analyse the subject from a time perspective requires a multi-country research project set-up adjustment of existing methodology and models such as gravity model to allow assessments and projections of FDIs based on the economic sizes and distance among n-countries and their interdependencies. Definitely, there is a research gap regarding FDI outflow from Asian countries to EU nations. One of the reasons for that could be the change of the FDI policies of Asian countries focusing more on regional investment markets than EU countries. This change is also influenced by the global economy lockdown in 2020 due to COVID-19 and investment screening restrictions.

Empirical results and discussion

Asian trade bloc magnified after 1980 with a strong link to the United States. Since then, the process of trade and investment Asian interregional and regional investment development was started. Both trade and investment stimulated the integration of Asian economies. One recent study has generalized this relationship and concluded that first trade expansion leads to FDI, and then the relationship is reversed and FDI leads to trade expansion (UNCTAD, 2001). Existing literature regarding FDIO from Asian countries to EU nations in the period 2010–2018 is rather limited, but there is a general consensus among economists regarding the positive and direct link of FDI and trade agreements on real GDP growth of the economy (Das, 2005). An interesting study on foreign direct outward investment from 34 OECD countries to 160 target countries in 2003–2011 is presented by S. Morris and J. Palakh from the Indian Institute of Management, but this study is based only on data from 2009 for all of the 34 countries (Morris & Palakh, 2016). Other study which covered 17 OECD countries analyses the impact of inward as well as outward FDI on industry performance by using Cobb–Douglas production function and does not specifically focus on OFDI from Asian countries (Bitzer & Görg, 2005). Other authors use Dunning's OLI framework to identify the country-specific macroeconomic growth drivers encouraging OFDI from India (Kaushal, 2018). There are some studies regarding EU–ASEAN integration using the gravity model to conclude that the EU was not focused directly on building a strong investment partnership with ASEAN (Plummer, 2002) and that the future economic and investment relation of EU should be built together with ASEAN (Welfens et al., 2006). According to the studies, ASEAN region members such as Singapore, Malaysia, Indonesia, Thailand, and the Philippines are prominent outflow investors in OECD countries, and they invest more than companies from India and China. These countries represent 21% of the total FDI outflow stock of ASEAN (Thomsen et al., 2011). Some of the authors show even adverse effects of FTAs on the FDI flows (Dee & Gali, 2003). According to the recent studies, value of FDI to Europe since 2000 started to decrease and amounted to 721 billion

USD while the FDI inflow trend to Asian countries increased (Wyrzykowska, 2010). Some authors focus on the analysis of the scale of intra- and interregional FDI flows between Asian developing countries and the EU and the role of the integration process with influence on FDI flow. Asian countries can be an alternative source of capital during a crisis time for new EU member countries. In general, integration processes in the EU and Asia helped to increase the FDI flow between Asian and EU countries (Witkowska, 2013). FDI outflow can have a significant impact on technology and productivity levels in host-country firms (Ha & Giroud,2015), as well as on local employment and skills levels (Bajo-Rubio & Díaz-Mora, 2015). The effects of FDI outflow can be also analysed from the FDI determinants and different types of FDI (vertical and horizontal) perspectives which have different effects on the host country (Dygas, 2020). Some authors point out that there is no clear convergence between free trade flows and FDIs that is why the choice of multinational companies with outsourcing and offshoring is still open (Welfens, 1997). There are also distinctions in the literature between capital mobility as mobile and immobile Schumpeter sectors where different types of FDIs are applicable (Klodt, 1993). Some authors underline the importance of different factors related to FDIs which impact the growth rate of the economy namely: human capital accumulation (Lucas, 1988), R&D expenditures (Grossman & Helpman, 1991). There is no much evidence in the literature specifying what percentage of FDIO from Asian countries went to the EU during 2010–2018 as the data are not consistent. Based upon key findings in the literature that the majority of FDIO in Asia has taken place mainly as internal investments within the Asian region for simplicity, it can be assumed that 10–15% of FDIO could flow to EU member countries during 2010–2018. Significant donors of FDIO in the EU can be France, the Netherlands, the UK, Germany, Italy, Switzerland, and Spain. Some studies are devoted to analyse the impact of Asian FDI outflow on specific EU countries such as the UK before Brexit (Stone, 1999), and, also according to some developed models, even EU integration and Eurozone did not help enough to impact EU members' capacity to attract FDIs from non-EU countries, it rather helped to increase FDIs from other EU member states by almost 44% as the result of joining the EU single market and almost by 74% by joining Euro-zone (Carril-Caccia & Pavlova, 2018). Further integration within the CEE region and as a result forming Visegrad Group (V4) helped to boost FDIO from Asia, but a lack of clear economic policy from V4 on how to use a potential of Asian trade relations made the entire opportunity suspended. The emergence of COVID-19 disrupted main regional integration processes globally and has made Asian countries, excluding China, to focus more on FDI inflow and rebuilding their own economies. In the next part of this chapter, the impact of FDIO from Asia on EU countries is analysed. Since 1980, Asia was an important trade region for FDIO which mainly was built on M&A rather than on greenfield projects which consisted of 80% of the total Asian FDIO (Mukhopadhyay & Thomassin, 2010). Asia and the EU reached close to 90 billion USD cross-border FDI annually (2015–2017), and China, Hong Kong, India, South Korea, and Japan were the biggest investors in the EU, Japan and China amounting their FDIs to 12 billion USD (Neves et al., 2019). In Table 9.1, there are FDIO values presented per each

Table 9.1 FDI outflow from Asian countries in 2010–2018 in billion USD

	2010	*2011*	*2012*	*2013*	*2014*	*2015*	*2016*	*2017*	*2018*
Bangladesh	66	297	289	547	42	60	41	127	15
Bhutan	28	33	54	22	22	4	−7	−10	6
Cambodia	21	29	36	62	82	88	79	115	124
China	57 954	48 421	64 963	72 971	123 130	174 391	216 424	138 293	96 472
Hong Kong SAR, China	98 431	95 906	88 123	83 328	140 892	78 515	75 552	101 762	75 012
India	15 968	12 608	8 553	1 765	11 686	7 514	5 047	11 090	11 418
Indonesia	4 186	9 037	7 485	11 112	10 388	9 075	−11 594	2 008	6 399
Japan	79 657	116 835	117 632	155 685	137 924	138 415	178 610	173 839	159 099
Korea, Dem. People's Rep.	14	103	205	119	102	79	89	−13	52
Korea, Rep. (South Korea)	28 222	29 648	30 599	28 318	27 999	23 687	29 890	34 069	38 220
Malaysia	15 349	18 108	16 897	13 408	16 060	10 542	10 097	5 608	5 716
Mongolia	62	95	65	41	107	11	14	49	28
Myanmar	6 669	1 118	497	584	946	2 824	2 989	4 341	3 554
Pakistan	47	62	77	212	122	25	52	52	9
Singapore	35 407	31 900	20 480	45 279	52 477	45 223	39 782	43 696	36 331
Thailand	8 131	7 176	14 261	12 121	5 742	4 991	13 362	18 632	20 696
Vietnam	900	950	1 200	1 956	1 150	1 100	1 000	480	598
World	1 818 332	2 221 485	1 778 598	2 053 810	1 803 508	2 160 695	2 103 150	1 877 386	921 028

Source: The World Bank, data.worldbank.org

Asian country in the period 2010–2018. Based on the information in the previous part of the chapter, it can be assumed that 10–15% of these stated amounts account for FDI in EU-28. Major important trade partners and direct foreign investors in the EU is China with Hong Kong.

According to the European Commission, China accounted for 19.4% of its total export in 2005 and also export for the EU to China increased and reached 43.5 billion EUR in 2005, and the EU trade deficit with China was slightly more than 74 billion EUR in 2005 (EC, 2007). Data presented in Table 9.1 showed also a leading position of China and Hong Kong in FDIO among Asian countries during 2010–2018. According to the FDI report 2020, China retained also its leading FDIO investment position in the Asia-Pacific region in 2019 with 61.4 billion USD (23% of FDI Asia-Pacific market share) before Japan with FDIO in the same region with 43 billion USD although Japan had more FDIO projects than China in 2019 (fDi, 2020). Table 9.2 presents the number of FDI inflow projects into the EU with Poland in the fifth position with an FDIO of 21.8 billion USD.

Looking at the data in Table 9.2, the UK was a leader in receiving FDI from other countries in 2019, but comparing data from 2018, the number of projects (1290), capital investment (35.7 billion USD), and the number of jobs created decreased. It was mainly due to the process of Brexit and the future UK investment uncertainty. In Table 9.3 it is viewed from the other side of European countries that received FDI from chosen Asian countries China and Japan in the 2010–2018 period. The main overall problem is data availability for the whole period of 2010–2018. That makes the entire empirical study limited, but, based even on the latest OECD available data, it can be stated that the main leaders of FDI inflow stock from Europe based only on China and Japan are the UK, Germany, the Netherlands, France, and Belgium with a dominance of Japanese foreign direct investments stocks value in these countries over the analysed period. Japan was also pointed out as the FDI outflow leader (143 billion USD, 2.9% of

Table 9.2 FDIO into EU-chosen countries in 2019, ranked by number of projects

	Country	*Project Numbers*	*Europe Market Share in %*	*FDIO Value in Billion USD*
1	The UK	1271	20%	32.3
2	Germany	702	9%	19.2
3	Spain	658	9%	19.1
4	France	500	7%	15.7
5	**Poland**	**373**	**10%**	**21.8**
6	The Netherlands	314	5%	10.8
7	Ireland	203	5%	11
8	Belgium	182	4%	8.1
9	Hungary	>182	3%	7.5

Source: Based on data from fDi (2020) Report.

Table 9.3 FDI inflow stocks from China and Japan to Europe in the period 2010–2018 (in million USD)

Country	*China*	*Japan*	*Total*
Czech Republic	3 487	16 322	19 809
Austria	4 841	17 762	22 603
Belgium	−4 612	98 412	93 800
Germany	37 002	193 957	230 959
Denmark	1 216	8 628	9 844
Spain	5 965	17 260	23 225
Estonia	41	688	729
Finland	20 909	6 497	27 406
France	34 655	124 249	158 904
The UK	16 247	417 450	433 697
Greece	744	260	1 004
Hungary	7 141	10 377	17 518
Ireland	5 235	13 919	19 154
Island	667	0	667
Italy	16 011	44 307	60 318
Lithuania	131	158	289
Luxemburg	29 867	25 413	55 280
Latvia	397	1	398
The Netherlands	10 202	108 971	119 173
Poland	4 567	27 605	32 172
Portugal	9 919	2 818	12 737
Slovakia	186	490	676
Slovenia	411	798	1 209
Sweden	27 314	22 670	49 984
Total	232 543	1 159 012	1 391 555

Source: Own calculation based on OECD data 2010–2018, www.data.oecd.org

*Negative FDI net inflow stock means that divestment is greater than investment

GDP) in 2018 in the UNCTAD report, while China's FDIO value was 130 billion USD and 1% of GDP in 2018 (UNCTAD, 2019).

Most of the important global transnational companies were active in those countries in the EU, which had the biggest FDI inflow in Europe during the 2010–2018 period. Motives for outward investment differ by firm, sector, country, and ownership. They include many of those typically associated with FDIO such as market access, low-cost labour, resource seeking, and technology sourcing. Besides China and Japan, other Asian countries as well, especially from the ASEAN region such as Singapore, Malaysia, and Thailand, played a significant role in providing foreign capital to EU economies especially the United Kingdom. Singapore was the strongest investor in 2009 (62% of ASEAN's outflow stock)

Table 9.4 FDI outflow percentage from chosen Asian countries to Europe and Asia including ASEAN region, 2009, in million USD

	Europe	*Asia and ASEAN*
Singapore	13%	53%
Malaysia	12%	44%
Thailand	3%	80%

Source: Own calculations based on Thomsen, S., Misuzu, O., Boram, L., 2011. The Evolving Role of Southeast Asia in Global FDI Flows, Asie.Vision 40., Ifri Centre for Asian Studies, June 2011., pp. 44–46

as it was supported by its governmental programs since 1988. Singapore's FDI outflow was focused on two main industries: Manufacturing (low labour cost and market access seeking) and financial and insurance services (market seeking). The state-linked company example investing heavily overseas also in Europe (mainly in the UK) can be Temasek Holdings which owns and manages a net portfolio worth of 313 billion USD. Malaysia could increase its FDI outflow in 2008 due to regional structural changes and government support to encourage companies to go global. The state-owned Malaysian companies such as Petronas and Khazanah Nasional Berhad invested in oil and gas and agriculture industries. Thailand is still a minor direct investor in Europe. The main reason for that was a lack of strong ownership advantages of Thai investors (Hill & Jongwanich, 2009). The FDIO data for Singapore, Malaysia, and Thailand are presented in Table 9.4.

The conclusion from Table 9.4 can be the fact that majority of FDIs in Asia are interregional type within Asia. It depends on EU policy if that characteristic of FDIs can be changed or not. It should be in interests of both sides of the EU and ASEAN to mutually benefit from and have counterparts to Chinese investments in the EU. The projections of COVID-19 and Brexit impacts on Asia's FDIO globally were presented further in this chapter.

Discussion on the projection of COVID-19 and Brexit impact on Asia's FDIO globally

FDI outflow from Asia and the Pacific decreased by 8% to 522.3 billion USD in 2018; the region nonetheless increased its share of global FDI outflows from 40% in 2017 to 52% in 2018. The East and North-East Asia subregion was the largest source of intraregional greenfield FDI outflows in 2018, followed by the ASEAN subregion. East and North-East Asia accounted for 66% of all intraregional greenfield FDI outflows, while ASEAN was responsible for 23% (ESCAP, 2019). Due to an unexpected economic downturn caused by coronavirus SARS-CoV2, the FDI outflow is expected to decrease stronger (even up to 40% according to UNCTAD), but there are no official data yet for the 2020–2022 period. India was very badly hit due to the country lockdown. India's economic growth was projected as negative at −3.1% for 2020 by Moody's Investors Service as the addition of some military tensions at the border with China could lead to geopolitical risk in Asia. India's overseas direct investment (ODI) dipped by 62% in April 2020 according to the Reserve Bank of India (RBI).[1] FDI outflow from Asian countries more likely will be directed regionally in Asia and also to some chosen destinations in Europe like the UK. Some studies projected that Brexit will cut FDI inflow to the UK by even 12–28% (Dhingra et al., 2016). Due to Brexit, 70 recorded companies relocated their operations from the UK to other European countries like Germany, the Netherlands, France, Spain, and Ireland (fDi, 2020). Eastern Europe can also "benefit" from this situation as well while mass production can be moved from China to India, Japan, and the CEE region. For example Japanese FDI outflow to Poland, including recent Toyota's project localized in Jelcz-Laskowice, the total level of investments in both Toyota Motor Manufacturing Poland plants will increase to nearly 1.2 billion EUR in 2022 and the total employment will increase to approximately 3000 people.[2]. The future of FDI outflow to EU countries will be much more complicated for the investors so some delays in direct investment transactions between EU and non-EU countries should be expected. Before the coronavirus pandemic in March 2019, European Parliament and European Council set up the screening framework for all EU member states regarding FDI inflow to the EU from the non-EU countries including Asia. This Regulation (EU) 2019/452 in Article 4 specifies factors that need to be taken into consideration by all EU member states concerning FDI inflow to the EU and whether it affects security or public order. Besides that, each EU member state according to Article 5 of this regulation by 31 March of each year has to submit an annual report covering the preceding calendar year to the Commission, which shall include aggregated information on foreign direct investments that took place in their territory. Besides such regulations, there is also MNEs side that has concerns regarding projections of FDI outflow to the other countries and stability of Global Value Chains (GVCs). Looking from this perspective, 1687 Asian MNEs made a revision of their 2020 earnings down by 15–30% and a decline of cross-border M&A's value by 40–70% due to the COVID-19 (UNCTAD, 2020). Those earning cuts impact FDI flow directly. Also, OECD's projections regarding FDI outflow from Asian countries are not positive, and, in the near future of 2020–2021, FDI flow will vary significantly in different countries and sectors depending much on public health and economic policy measures (even in OECD's optimistic scenario, FDI flow will fall by 30% in 2020 compared to 2019). Many companies in Asia are concerned with the stability of GVCs referring to Brexit and global trade tensions especially between the United States and China and also between the United States and Germany. Growing consumer demand and the rise of "new" emerging markets can lead to further GVC lengthening in the coming decade (OECD, 2020). It does not mean that nothing could be done in that pessimistic scenario. The big role is to be played by the multinational companies (MNCs) which are more R&D oriented than domestic firms and can help governments and Investment Promotion Agencies (IPAs) to stimulate FDIs and minimize the negative effects of pandemic COVID-19 in the global economy. The big barrier for MNCs is a growing bad debt which may prevent them from surviving the COVID-19 crisis and making new overseas investments. Besides that, foreign investors pulled back 26 billion USD from Asian countries (16 billion USD out of India) which accelerated a drop in trade volumes and recession in Asia (CRS, 2020). It relates to political decisions in many countries to lockdown their economies leading to global reset, which is not a subject of this chapter, but an important aspect for future projections. That is why it is just mentioned in this place.

During the COVID-19 isolation time, there were a vast number of webinars dedicated to the topic raised in this chapter. The important conclusion from several webinars such as the one organized by the Confederation of Indian Industry (www.cii.in) on the 18th of June 2020 was that Asia's FDI outflow to EU countries would be significantly reduced also due to GVCs decomposition, and mainly investments would take place in the Asian region. Another important conclusion is expected repositioning of India versus China in Asia and the leading role of India in FDI flow. China still has a dominant position in Asia and manages to drag most of the world's production including pharmaceuticals, medical products, and hardware, which were critical during fighting with COVID-19, to different countries. China increased its share in the global economy from 4% in 2003 (while fighting with SARS) to 20% in 2019 (fighting with COVID-19) making many countries dependant on China (Devonshire-Ellis, 2020). During COVID-19, some of the countries like Japan realized that dependency and took significant restrictive actions towards FDI outflow to China, heading as the result to economic tensions but not yet to a real decoupling (Kawashima, 2020). In 2020, Japan started to pull out its companies from China and also restrict FDI inflow from China to Japan as well. China, despite the coronavirus lockdown, has still a strong position with FDI in the EU even though China's FDI in EU-28 dropped by 33% in 2018 (Kratz et al., 2020). China's FDI inflow to EU countries was presented in Table 9.5.

Table 9.5 China's cumulative FDI in chosen EU countries in 2000–2019 in billion EUR

Country	*FDI in Billion EUR*
The UK	50.3
Germany	22.7
Italy	15.9
France	14.4
Finland	12.0
The Netherlands	10.2
Hungary	**2.4**
Poland	**1.2**

Source: Based on the Mercator Institute for China Studies, MERICS, 2019 update

The results in Table 9.5 show the countries with the highest cumulative Chinese FDIs, namely the UK, Germany, Italy, France, and the Netherlands. Recent data have shown some change in trends in Chinese FDI outflow to Europe. Northern-Europe countries like Finland, Sweden, and Ireland received the most FDI from China in 2019. It was mainly done by M&A of European companies by Chinese capital [examples: Anta's acquisition of Amer (Finland) or China Evergrande acquisition of Nevs (Sweden)]. China to secure its position due to some FDI restrictions set by European Parliament and European Council started to use alternative approaches such as establishing R&D collaboration with EU companies, governments, and universities (Kratz et al., 2020). Those R&D partnerships are not covered and regulated in the FDI-screening framework which may be overused by China for technology and knowledge transfer from the EU especially to the Chinese military sector. Poland and Hungary were shown in Table 9.5 as the contrast to Western EU countries regarding FDIs. Those big differences between China's FDI values in western EU countries and CEE region countries could be explained by the fact that Polish and Hungarian governments were not that attractive for China and also not that open with investment policy towards Asian economies as other EU members. Poland still does not have a clear policy regarding trade and investment development with Asian countries, which impacts the trade and investment results. EU countries between 2015 and 2016 allocated 1 billion EUR government contracts with Chinese companies mainly for infrastructure and construction (Wagner, 2018). That also explains the strong position of China in the EU to pave the way for China Belt and Road Initiative in 2019. This project is very large investment-wise, and it is also a part of the new international economic order supported by the Chinese government (Strittmatter, 2020). This initiative is only mentioned in this chapter as the example of transferring a position of China to investment hegemony in the EU, which also showed to the EU its other negative face during coronavirus where the concentration of production in China blocked EU countries to fight with COVID-19 without a "Chinese support". The EU implementing FDI-screening framework and imposing some restrictions on Chinese FDI needs, in the future, to develop trade and investment relations with India and ASEAN member countries to overcome the losses after coronavirus economy lockdown. It seems as of the current situation that there is no better alternative.

Network analysis model

A simple static undirected network model of the outward FDI from selected Asian economies to selected European economies was constructed. For the sake of visualization, the edges in the network have directional arrows symbolizing outward FDI; however, all our measures used in the calculations treat them as undirected. The analysis looks at the data for the 2018 FDI position which comes from OECD Statistics (https://stats.oecd.org/). OECD defines a position as "the value of the stock of direct investments held at the end of the reference period (typically year or quarter)." Missing or negative values were substituted with an edge weight of 0.

There are 13 selected source Asian economies and 27 host European economies. The graph has 40 nodes (representing selected economies) and 211 edges (representing links between nodes). The network density of the graph is relatively high at 0.271 (1 indicates a complete graph with every possible edge). The average degree is 5.275 (the average number of connections of every node).

To quantify the network importance and patterns, the weighted undirected PageRank and modularity class of every node using Gephi were calculated (open-source network modelling software). PageRank is a popular measure of network importance/centrality, commonly used in network methodology studies. The following algorithms in the analysis were employed: Modularity class (communities of nodes) is determined by Blondel et al. (2008); modularity class resolution (the size of communities) is determined by Lambiotte et al. (2014); and PageRank (network importance of a node) is determined by Brin and Page (1998).

Table 9.6 shows the PageRank scores for the network (a higher number indicates higher importance). The highest scores for the Asian economies are for

Table 9.6 Network importance of selected economies

Economy	*Category*	*PageRank (weighted, undirected)*	*Economy*	*Category*	*PageRank (weighted, undirected)*
Japan	Asia (source)	0.1903	**Thailand**	Asia (source)	0.0103
The United Kingdom	Europe (host)	0.1032	**Czech Republic**	Europe (host)	0.0097
Hong Kong	Asia (source)	0.0940	**Norway**	Europe (host)	0.0090
Luxembourg	Europe (host)	0.0864	**Turkey**	Europe (host)	0.0086
China	Asia (source)	0.0687	**Slovak Republic**	Europe (host)	0.0080
Germany	Europe (host)	0.0477	**Malaysia**	Asia (source)	0.0080
Singapore	Asia (source)	0.0428	**Portugal**	Europe (host)	0.0075
France	Europe (host)	0.0322	**Denmark**	Europe (host)	0.0054
Switzerland	Europe (host)	0.0318	**Vietnam**	Asia (source)	0.0047
South Korea	Asia (source)	0.0313	**Indonesia**	Asia (source)	0.0046
Netherlands	Europe (host)	0.0287	**Greece**	Europe (host)	0.0045
India	Asia (source)	0.0189	**Philippines**	Asia (source)	0.0044
Belgium	Europe (host)	0.0182	**Finland**	Europe (host)	0.0043
Italy	Europe (host)	0.0149	**Slovenia**	Europe (host)	0.0042
Spain	Europe (host)	0.0139	**Latvia**	Europe (host)	0.0041
Hungary	Europe (host)	0.0135	**Iceland**	Europe (host)	0.0041
Sweden	Europe (host)	0.0130	**Estonia**	Europe (host)	0.0040
Ireland	Europe (host)	0.0124	**Bangladesh**	Asia (source)	0.0039
Poland	Europe (host)	0.0107	**Lithuania**	Europe (host)	0.0039
Austria	Europe (host)	0.0105	**Pakistan**	Asia (source)	0.0038

Source: Own calculations

Japan, Hong Kong, China, Singapore, South Korea, and India – representing a mix of large economies and important global financial centres. The highest scores for the European economies are for the UK, Luxembourg, Germany, France, Switzerland, and the Netherlands – representing advanced Western European countries, both large and small. The highest score for a Central and Eastern European economy is Hungary, followed by Poland. For the European economies, a high PageRank score indicates both larger gains from international FDI flows and higher importance for Asian multinational companies' investments.

Figure 9.1 represents the visualization of the network model. The node size is determined by its PageRank score, while its colour is determined by its modularity class (community). There are four communities in the network: Japan/India ("purple"), Hong Kong/Singapore ("orange"), China/South Korea ("green"), and Thailand ("blue"). A common modularity class can be interpreted as being a part of the same influence sphere when it comes to the outward FDI of Asian economies in Europe. Of the most important host economies (as measured by PageRank), the "purple" community has the UK, Germany, France, Switzerland, and the Netherlands; the "orange" community has Luxembourg, Spain, Austria, Denmark, and Greece; the "green" community has Italy, Hungary, Sweden, Ireland, and the Czech Republic; and the "blue" community has only Norway.

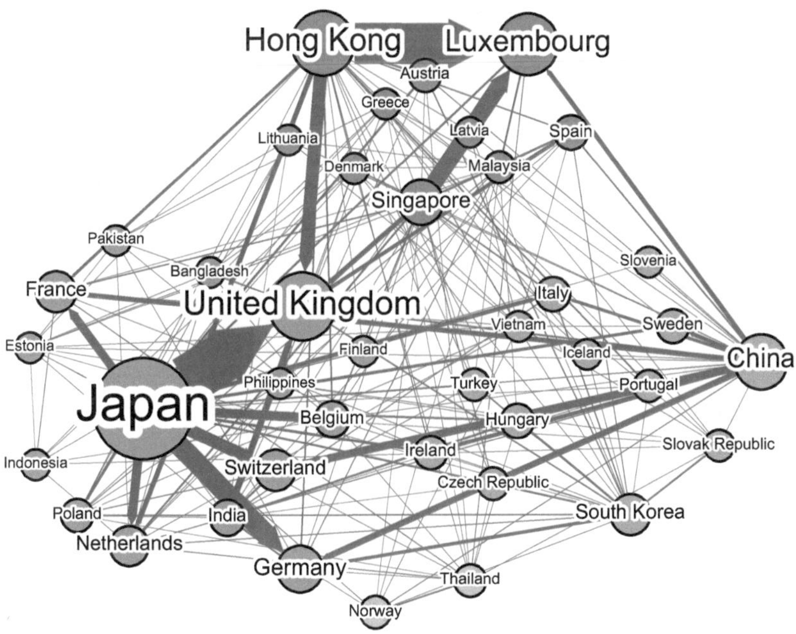

Figure 9.1 Network model of Asian outward FDI in Europe (2018, stock, selected economies)

Source: Own calculations

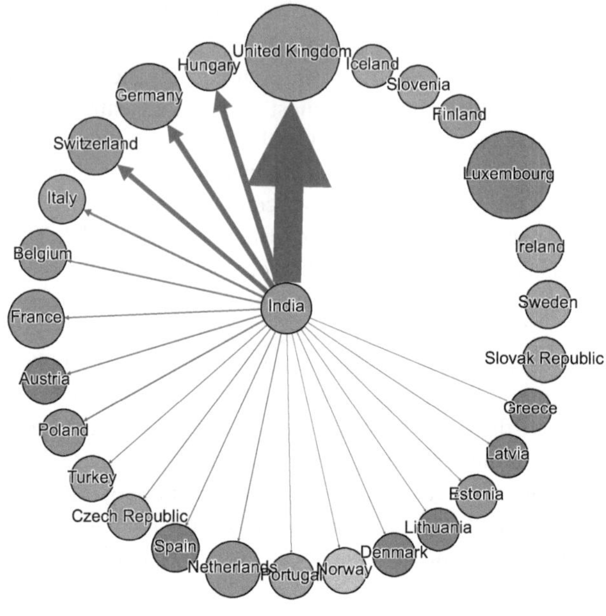

Figure 9.2 Network model of Asian outward FDI in Europe – India's FDI (2018, stock, selected economies)

Source: Own calculations.

Figure 9.2 is the filtered version of the network showing the hosts of Indian investments in Europe. It visualizes how the network would look like if other Asian economies are removed and left only India. The size and colour of the nodes are the same as in Figure 9.1. The most important destinations for India's outward FDI in Europe are the UK, Hungary, Germany, Switzerland, Italy, and Belgium.

Conclusion

The main part of this chapter is the analysis of Asian FDI outflow to the EU countries that identifies the main players and EU's top countries which benefited the most from them, like the UK, Germany, France, Italy, and the Netherlands. The chapter analyses mainly the period of 2010–2018 ex-ante COVID-19, while the projections for the FDI outflow from Asian countries to the EU are referring to the post-COVID-19 and post-Brexit future of 2020–2021.

Network analysis methodology provides new opportunities for economic research. According to the PageRank scores in our network, the most important nodes are large Asian economies (e.g. Japan and China), large European economies (e.g. the UK and Germany), and global financial centres (e.g. Hong Kong and Luxembourg). European economies' PageRank quantifies both their gains from international FDI flows and the importance for Asian multinationals. A common modularity class can be interpreted as being a part of the same influence sphere based on the FDI stock. The network analysis reveals four communities of network influence centred around Japan/India (e.g. the UK and Germany), Hong Kong/Singapore (e.g. Luxembourg and Spain), China/South Korea (e.g. Italy and Hungary), and Thailand (only Norway).

There are many post-COVID-19 scenarios and forecasts, but no one can be sure how exactly the FDI outflow from Asia to the EU will look like due to too many unknowns and structural changes in Asia and the EU as well. Existing projections are not optimistic due to the significant loss of FDIs globally as a consequence of Brexit and global economy lockdown, especially in India and other Asian countries. According to UNCTAD, FDIs globally will fall by 35–40% in 2020–2021 (UNCTAD, 2020b). Global FDI outflow decreased globally by 29% to 1 trillion USD in 2018, and the decrease was major in developed countries. Total FDI outflow from Asia declined by 8% keeping that region as the main source of FDI outflow (ESCAP, 2019). The Brexit and COVID-19 strongly impacted the further decrease trend and activities of transnational business. They showed how important it was for the EU to develop a new FDI policy with Asia, especially to tighten the investment relations with India and ASEAN member countries (mainly Singapore, Malaysia, and Thailand) as a counterpart to China.

China's post-COVID-19 FDI outflow projections are also unclear and questionable due to a lack of reliable data and information. It may be also a part of Chinese strategy to make the outlook picture blurred. Overall, it seems that China managed to get over the first wave of coronavirus suspiciously quickly and still has a strong economic position in the EU continuing its policy trying to get over European companies and win government contracts. Imposing FDI screening framework (Regulation (EU) 2019/452) should be a shield for the EU to prevent hostile takeovers of European companies by Chinese firms, as it was done during the recession in Europe during 2008–2012. The weak point of this shield is that R&D partnerships are not included so it can lead to the leakage of sensitive technologies and know-how. The EU needs to turn to India and ASEAN members and develop bilateral, strong trade and investment relations to counterpart China in the FDI area.

Notes

1 www.moneycontrol.com/news/business/economy/india-incs-foreign-direct-investment-dips-62-to-976-million-in-april-5294351.html, accessed 17 June 2020

2 https://auto.dziennik.pl/aktualnosci/artykuly/7726855,toyota-produkcja-polska-fabryka-jelcz-laskowice-silnik-hybryda.html, accessed 17 June 2020

Acknowledgements and conclusions

We would like to give full respect and pay our gratitude to all professors and researchers from China, Estonia, Iceland, India, Japan, Poland, and the United States who decided to share their knowledge and thoughts to create this book that is concentrated on Asian trade and investment in Europe with regional perspective.

The nine chapters give the answers to the questions formulated in preface of the book. Relevant case studies were also presented to underline the fact that Asia is the future of the global economy. COVID-19 with its lockdowns globally came out to be disruptive for global economy and especially international trade. The role of India is significant in stabilizing the situation in a digitized world where China's impact on production came to be unprecedently enormous. According to the main conclusion from the first chapter of this book, it needs to be stated that European countries of EFTA still require a trade with China, but there is a strong tendency during COVID-19 to have also a stronger counterparty for trade and investment which can be India and Japan. The results presented in Chapter 1 appear to be positive for exports from China, not export to China, or, in other words, FTAs stimulate flow from China, not flow to China. Based on that, it appears as if Free Trade Agreements between the EFTA countries and China will not pay off for the European countries. However, this holds for the period analysed and needs to be carefully considered when concluding the impact on current and later development. Also, in case of Baltic States, especially in case of Estonia, the demand for trade and investment with Asian countries is growing. Estonia can be the model example of the approach to develop bilateral relations with Asian economies like Japan and India. More attention today from Asian investors' side can bring in Europe Visegrad Group (V4) and 3SI with the investment opportunity especially *Via Carpatia*. Main issue to be solved is the limited space of autonomy in investment decisions of V4 and 3SI imposed by European Commission. V4 is perceived by Asian investors more to be like a political organization than a real business one, where the V4's leaders can make the investment decisions independently without the final decision of European Commission. This is important because future trade and investment relations between Asian and European countries would be multilateral. There are attempts from European Commission's side to keep the agreements with Asian countries as the Partnership Agreements (e.g. agreement between EU–India Connectivity Partnership). There are still significant barriers like legislation, required norms and standards in the trade and investment and investment risk increase related to global COVID-19 situation. Some of the agreements proposed by European Commission (e.g. EU–China agreement from 2020) are not accepted by all EU-27 member countries as it makes only leading EU countries beneficial, namely Germany and France. In spite of the fact that France and Germany are the strongest economies in EU, Indian investors from Tata Motors managed to invest in Slovakia in its new JLR plant in Nitra (Slovakia). As the matter of fact, recent events impacted the production of JLR plant. Brexit and disruption of deliveries of semiconductors and chips resulted in production stoppage and product sales fall of the JLR UK and worldwide.

The important question raised in this book is how do the trade and investment among Asian countries and European regions look like during COVID-19 time. The straight answer is that China still has hegemony position (e.g. considering the case of Tencent company described in Chapters 2 and 7), but the situation is changing due to the supply chain disruption caused by the COVID-19. It affected many sectors including European automotive where semiconductors and chips delivery problems made entire car production in many European countries come to a halt. There is a need for European countries to find the counterpart to China especially that geopolitical relations between the United States and China are getting rough since long time now. The further analysis and research should be done on the future role of Central and Eastern European countries in the development of bilateral trade and investment relations with Asian countries, especially with India, Japan, Thailand, Vietnam, and Indonesia. The relations with CEE countries can be beneficial also to Asian countries. In the case of India, it needs investments, technology, and a manufacturing ecosystem to employ millions of its young people and improve their living standards. The alignment of India with the United States and a stronger cooperation with V4 and 3SI countries can be a right move.

References

Acemoglu, D., & Robinson, J. A. (2019). *The Narrow Corridor* (States, Societies and the Fate of Liberty). London: Viking.

Alison, Tudor-Ackroyd. (2020). China foils world's largest stock listing 48 hours before kick-off as Ant Group delays market debut in Shanghai and Hong Kong. *South China Morning Post*. www.scmp.com/business/companies/article/3108309/shanghais-stock-market-operator-calls-halt-ant-groups-imminent. Accessed 10.05.2021.

Anderson, J. E. (1979). A theoretical foundation for the gravity equation. *The American Economic Review*, 69(1), 106–116.

Antràs, P., & De Gortari, A. (2020). On the geography of global value chains. *Econometrica*, 88(4), 1553–1598.

Arjun, K., & Cheng, E. (2021). The latest target of China's tech regulation blitz: Algorithms. *CNBC*. www.cnbc.com/2021/09/03/chinas-tech-regulation-turns-to-algorithms.html. Accessed 10.05.2021.

Arthur, W. B. (1989). Competing technologies, increasing returns, and lock-in by historical events. *Economic Journal*, 99(394), 116–131.

Arthur, W. B. (1996). Increasing returns and the new world of business. *Harvard Business Review*, 74(4), 100.

Aspengren, H. C., Liden, E., & Nordenstam, A. (2021). Circles of EU-India engagement: How member states cooperate with India on global issues. *The Swedish Institute of International Affairs*, Paper 1/2021, pp. 7–9. www.ui.se/globalassets/ui.se-eng/publications/ui-publications/2021/ui-paper-no.-1-2021.pdf. Accessed 13.07.2021.

Aversa, P., Haefliger, S., Hueller, F., & Reza, D. G. (2020). Customer complementarity in the digital space: Exploring Amazon's business model diversification. *Long Range Planning*, 101985.

Azad, S., & Gupta, A. (2011). Evaluating India's strategic partnerships using analytic hierarchy process. *IDSA Comment*, September 17. www.idsa.in/idsacomments/EvaluatingIndiasStrategicPartnershipsusingAnalyticHierarhyProcess_agupta_170911. Accessed 13.07.2021.

Bagwell, X., & Staiger, Y. (2005). Erratum to multilateral trade negotiations, bilateral opportunism and the rules of GATT/WTO. *Journal of International Economics*, 67(2), 268–294.

Bahmani-Oskooee, M., Bose, N., & Zhang, Y. (2018). Asymmetry cointegration, nonlinear ARDL and the J-curve: China versus her 21 trading partners. *Emerging Markets Finance and Trade*, 54, 3130–3150.

Bahmani-Oskooee, M., Harvey, H., & Hegerty, S. W. (2017). The Japanese trade balance and asymmetric effects of yen fluctuations: Evidence using nonlinear methods. *The Journal of Economic Asymmetries*, 15, 56–63.

Bahmani-Oskooee, M., & Hegerty, S. W. (2007). Exchange rate volatility and trade flows: A review article. *Journal of Economic Studies*, 34, 211–255.

Bahmani-Oskooee, M., & Hegerty, S. W. (2009). The effects of exchange-rate volatility on commodity trade between the U.S. and Mexico. *Southern Economic Journal*, 79, 1019–1044.

Bahmani-Oskooee, M., & Ratha, A. (2004). The J-curve: A literature review. *Applied Economics*, 36, 1377–1398.

Bahmani-Oskooee, M., & Saha, S. (2017). Non-linear ARDL approach and bilateral J-curve: India vs. her trading partners. *Contemporary Economic Policy*, 35(3), 472–483.

Bahmani-Oskooee, M., & Saha, S. (2021). On the asymmetric effects of exchange rate volatility on the trade flows of India with each of its fourteen partners. *Macroeconomics and Finance in Emerging Economies*, 14(1), 66–85.

Bai, J., & Perron, P. (1998). Estimating and testing linear models with multiple structural changes. *Econometrica*, 66(1), 47–78.

Bajo-Rubio, O., & Díaz-Mora, C. (2015). On the employment effects of outward FDI: The case of Spain, 1995–2011. *Applied Economics*, 47(21), 2127–2141.

Baldwin, C. Y., & Woodard, C. J. (2009). The architecture of platforms: A unified view. *Platforms, Markets and Innovation*, 32, 19–44.

Baldwin, D. (1993). *Neo-Realism and Neo-Liberalism: The Contemporary Debate*. New York: Columbia University Press.

Basu, N. (2021). "Want India to be more open in trade with Poland, will boost investment": Envoy Burakowski. *The Print 2021*, February 8. https://theprint.in/diplomacy/want-india-to-be-more-open-in-trade-with-poland-will-boost-investment-envoy-burakowski/600330/. Accessed 12.07.2021.

Becker, W., Dominguez-Torreiro, M., Neves, A. R., Tacao Moura, C. J., & Saisana, M. (2019). *Exploring ASEM Sustainable Connectivity: What Brings Asia and Europe Together?*. ISBN 978-92-79-99726-6. doi:10.2760/738153. PUBSY JRC112998.

Benkovskis, K. E. A. (2019). Export and productivity in global value chains: Comparative evidence from Latvia and Estonia. *Review of World Economics*, 1–21.

Bergstrand, J. H. (1985). The gravity equation in international trade: Some microeconomic foundations and empirical evidence. *The Review of Economics and Statistics*, 67, 474–481.

Bergstrand, J. H. (1989). The generalized gravity equation, monopolistic competition, and the factor-proportions theory in international trade. *The Review of Economics and Statistics*, 71(1), 143–153.

Bhasin, H. (2018). *SWOT Analysis of Jaguar: Jaguar SWOT Analysis*. [Online] Marketing91. www.marketing91.com/swot-analysis-jaguar. Accessed 05.10.2021.

Biswas, P. K., & Dygas, R. (2021). *Asian Foreign Direct Investment in Europe*. London and New York: Routledge, Taylor&Francis Group.

Bitzer, J., & Görg, H. (2005). The impact of FDI on industry performance. Research Paper, No. 2005 09, Leverhulme Centre for Research on Globalisation and Economic Policy, University of Nottingham, Nottingham.

Blondel, V. D., Guillaume, J.-L., Lambiotte, R., & Lefebvre, E. (2008). Fast unfolding of communities in large networks. *Journal of Statistical Mechanics: Theory and Experiment*, 2008(10), P10008. https://doi.org/10.1088/1742-5468/2008/10/P10008

Bollerslev, T. (1986). Generalized autoregressive conditional heteroscedasticity. *Journal of Econometrics*, 31, 307–327.

Bolt. (2017). *Taxify Partnering with Didi Chuxing*. https://blog.bolt.eu/en/taxify-partnering-with-didi-chuxing/

Brands, H., & Beckley, M. (2021). China is a declining power: And that's the problem. *Foreign Policy*, September 24.

Brenton, P., & Manzocchi, S. (2002). *Enlargement, Trade and Investment*. Cheltenham: Edward Elgar Publishing.

Brin, S., & Page, L. (1998). The anatomy of a large-scale hypertextual Web search engine. *Computer Networks and ISDN Systems*, 30(1–7), 107–117. https://doi.org/10.1016/S0169-7552(98)00110-X

Brynjolfsson, E., Hu, Y. J., & Smith, M. D. (2006). From niches to riches: Anatomy of the long tail. *Sloan Management Review*, 47(4), 67–71.

Business Facilities. (2018). *Google Investing $600M in Oklahoma Data Center*, February 20. https://businessfacilities.com/2018/02/google-investing-600m-mayes-county-oklahoma-data-center/

Capital Economics. (2021). CE Projections for US and China GDP.

Carril-Caccia, F., & Pavlova, E. (2018). Foreign direct investment and its drivers: A global and EU perspective. *ECB Economic Bulletin*, Issue 4/2018. www.ecb.europa.eu/pub/economicbulletin/html/eb201804.en.html#IDofOverview_Eb1. Accessed 21.06.2020.

Cernat, L. (2021). We need to talk trade and technology. *ECIPE Policy Brief*, 8, 1–10.

Cernat, L., & Kutlina-Dimitrova, Z. (2014). Thinking in a box: A "mode 5" approach to service trade. *Journal of World Trade*, 48(6).

Cerulus, L. (2020). Coronavirus forces Europe to Confront China dependency. *Politico*, March 6. www.politico.eu/article/coronavirus-emboldens-europes-supply-chain-security-hawks/

Chandler, A. D., Jr. (1962). *Strategy and Structure*. Cambridge, MA: MIT Press.

Cheng, I., & Wall, H. (2004). Controlling for heterogeneity in gravity models of trade and integration, 1999–010E. *Federal Reserve Bank of St. Louis Review*, 87(Jan), 49–63.

Chowdhury, Abdur R. (1993). Does exchange rate volatility depress trade flows? Evidence from error-correction models. *The Review of Economics and Statistics*, 75, 700–706.

Cioffi, J. W., Kenney, M., & Zysman, J. (2021). *Platform Power and Regulatory Politics: Polanyi for the 21st Century*. Available at SSRN 3859075.

Coe, N. M., & Yang, C. (2021). Mobile gaming production networks, platform business groups, and the market power of China's Tencent. *Annals of the American Association of Geographers*, 1–24.

Cooney, K., & Sato, Y. (2009). *The Rise of China and International Security: America and Asia Respond*. London: Routledge.

CRS. (2020). *Congressional Research Service, Global Economic Effects of COVID-19*, updated June 19, p. 3. https://crsreports.congress.govR46270. Accessed 01.07.2020.

Cushman, D. O. (1992). The effects of real exchange rate risk on international trade. *Journal of International Economics*, 15, 45–63.

Das, D. K. (2005). *Trade, Competitiveness and Foreign Investment and the Linkages among Them*. Asian Economy and Finance, Springer, pp. 147–199.

Dee, P., & Gali, J. (2003). The trade and investment effects of preferential trading arrangements. NBER Working Paper No. 10160.

Dettoni, J. (2016). *Will Jaguar Land Rover Deal Lead Slovakia into a Golden Age of FDI?* www.fdiintelligence.com/article/66026. Accessed 04.10.2021.

Devonshire-Ellis, Ch. (2020). China's COVID-19 recovery: What lies ahead for foreign investors. *China Briefing*, March 9. www.china-briefing.com/news/chinas-covid-19-recovery-what-lies-ahead-for-foreign-investors-op-ed/. Accessed 19.06.2020.

Dhingra, S., Ottaviano, G., Sampson, T., & Van Reenen, J. (2016). The impact of Brexit on foreign investment in the UK. CEP Brexit Analysis, No 3, Centre for Economic Performance, London School of Economics.

Doktor.se. (2021). Digital healthcare start-up Doctor.se secures up to E29.5 million in investment from Tencent. July 16. https://doktor.se/digital-healthcare-startup-doktor-se-secures-up-to-e29-5-million-in-investment-from-tencent/

Dunning, J. H. (1977). Trade, location of economic activity and the MNE: A search for an eclectic approach. In B. Ohlin, P.-O. Hesselborn, & P. M. Wijkman (Eds.), *The International Allocation of Economic Activity*, Chap. 12. London: Macmillan.

Dygas, R. (2020). Determinants of foreign direct investment outflow from India to Poland. *International Journal of Management and Economics*, 56(2), 1–9.

Dygas, R. (2021). Chapter 16: Poland's bilateral economic ties with India in the context of the economic potential of its trading partners. In A. M. Kowalski & M. M. Weresa (Eds.), *Poland Competitiveness Report 2021* (pp. 293–316). Warsaw: SGH Warsaw School of Economics Publishing Office.

Dzienis, A. M. (2021). Japanese FDI in Poland. In P. K. Biswas & R. Dygas (Eds.), *Asian Foreign Direct Investment in Europe*, Chap. 5. Abingdon: Routledge.

EC. (2007). Annual report on the Euro area 2007. European Commission. Brussels: Directorate-General for Economic and Financial Affairs, pp. 42–43.

EC. (2019). 2019 report on implementation of EU free trade agreements 1 January–31 December 2018. Report from the Commission to European Parliament, the Council, the European Economic and Social Committee of the Regions on Implementation of Free Trade Agreements 1 January 2018–31 December 2018, European Commission 2019. https://trade.ec.europa.eu/doclib/docs/2019/october/tradoc_158387.pdf. Accessed 12.05.2020.

ECFR. (2020). The Meaning of systemic rivalry: Europe and China beyond the pandemic. *ECFR*, June 26. www.ecfr.eu/publications/summary/the_meaning_of_systemic_rivalry_europe_and_china_beyond_the_pandemic

Economist. (2021). The Thales of economics. September 18. Print edition.

EEAS. (2013). EU-China 2020 strategic agenda for cooperation, press and information team of the delegation of the European Union to China. *European Union External Action Service*. http://eeas.europa.eu/archives/docs/china/docs/eu-china_2020_strategic_agenda_en.pdf. Accessed 12.05.2020.

EEAS. (2018). EU-India trade and investment, press and information team of the delegation of the European Union to India and Bhutan. *European External Action Service*. https://eeas.europa.eu/sites/eeas/files/trade.pdf. Accessed 12.05.2020.

Egger, P. (2000). A note on the proper econometric specification of the gravity equation. *Economics Letters*, 66(1), 25–31.

Eicher, T. S., & Henn, C. (2011). In search of WTO, trade effects: Preferential trade agreements promote trade strongly, but unevenly. *Journal of International Economics*, 83(2), 137–153.

Eisenmann, T., Parker, G., & Van Alstyne, M. (2011). Platform envelopment. *Strategic Management Journal*, 32(12), 1270–1285.

Erixon, F. (2021). *Time for a New Industrial Policy*. [Online]. https://ecipe.org/blog/time-for-a-new-industrial-policy/. Accessed 15.09.2021.

ERR. (2020). Elisa CEO hits out at ministry Huawei tech ban draft. *ERR News*. https://news.err.ee/1117620/elisa-ceo-hits-out-at-ministry-huawei-tech-ban-draft

ESCAP. (2019). Asia Pacific trade and investment trends 2019/2020. Foreign Direct Investment Trends and Outlook in Asia and the Pacific, the Economic for Social Commission for Asia and the Pacific. www.unescap.org/resources/foreign-direct-investment-trends-and-outlook-asia-and-pacific-20192020. Accessed 12.05.2020.

Estonian Business Registry. (2021). *Data on Bolt*. Tallinn, Estonia.

EU. (2018). EU strategy on India. Joint Communication to European Parliament and Council, adopted November 20, Brussels, European Union. http://euindiabusinesssupport.eu/wp-content/uploads/2019/08/India-Strategy-and-Council-conclusions-layouted.pdf. Accessed 12.05.2020.

EU. (2019). Regulation (EU) 2019/452 of the European Parliament and of the Council of 19 March 2019 establishing a framework for the screening of foreign direct investments into the Union. *Official Journal of the European Union*. http://data.europa.eu/eli/reg/2019/452/oj. Accessed 06.05.2020.

Europe. (2021). January 20. https://europa.eu/.

European Commission. (2020). *The Digital Economy and Society Index*. Brussels, Belgium: European Commission.

European Free Trade Association. (2021). January 20. www.efta.int.

Europium, Institute for European Policy. (2021). *Report: V4 and Larger Regional Platforms: Convergence or Competition?* April 21, pp. 1–4. https://europeum.org/data/articles/report-brusel-tvb.pdf. Accessed 06.07.2021.

Eurostat. (2017). *Compilers Guide for Statistics on Services Trade by Enterprise Characteristics (STEC)* (1st ed.). Luxembourg: Publications Office of the European Union.

Evans, D. S. (2003). The antitrust economics of multi-sided platform markets. *Yale Journal of Regulation*, 20(2), 325–381.

fDi. (2020). *The fDi Report 2020 Global Greenfield Investment Trends*. http://report.fdiintelligence.com/files/ThefDiReport2020.pdf. Accessed 19.05.2020.

Feng, C., & Chan, B. (2021). Beijing names WeChat and other apps for data flaws and shuts down fan club apps, as scrutiny ratchets up. *South China Morning Post*. www.scmp.com/tech/policy/article/3145645/beijing-names-wechat-and-other-apps-data-flaws-and-shuts-down-fan-club. Accessed 10.05.2021.

Financial Times. (2020). FDI European cities and regions of the future 2020/21.

FNSR, Foundation for National Security Research. (2011). *India's Strategic Partners: A Comparative Assessment*. New Delhi.

Gambini, G. R. I., & Kerner, R. (2015). *USA-EU: International Trade and Investment Statistics*. Luxembourg: Eurostat.

Gawer, A. (2014). Bridging differing perspectives on technological platforms: Toward an integrative framework. *Research Policy*, 43(7), 1239–1249.

Geloso, G. (2015). *Services Trade Restriction Index (STRI): Scoring and Weighting Methodology*. Paris: OECD Publishing.

Goldstein, M., & Khan, M. (1985). Income and price effect in foreign trade. In R. W. Jones & P. B. Kenen (Eds.), *Handbook of International Economics* (pp. 1042–1099). North Holland, Amsterdam: Elsevier.

Gratius, S. (2011). Can EU strategic partnerships deepen multilateralism? FRIDE Working Paper No. 109, September, p. 7.

Grossman, G. M., & Helpman, E. (1991). *Innovation and Growth in the Global Economy*. Cambridge, MA: MIT Press.

Ha, H. J., & Giroud, A. (2015). Competence-creating subsidiaries and FDI technology spill overs. *International Business Review*, 24(4), 605–614.

Haeck, P. (2021). China's Tencent goes on a European shopping spree. *Politico*. www.politico.eu/article/china-tencent-video-game-industry-investment-europe/. Accessed 10.05.2021.

Hagiu, A. (2009). Multi-sided platforms: From micro-foundations to design and expansion strategies. Harvard Business School Strategy Unit Working Paper, pp. 09–115.

Hämäläinen, V.-P. (2021). Entinen kansanedustaja Antero Vartia saa syytteen Compensate-säätiön toiminnasta – "Pääasia että saadaan ratkaistu. June 3. Helsinki, Finland: Yle. https://yle.fi/uutiset/3-11963617

Hegerty, S. W. (2020). Housing loans and domestic credit in the Baltic states and Poland: Structural breaks and macroeconomic determinants. *Journal of Economics and Management*, 42(4), 48–69.

Heng, S. (2015). What happens when a Chinese Tycoon stands up against the government? *Forbes*. www.forbes.com/sites/hengshao/2015/01/29/what-happens-when-a-chinese-tycoon-stands-up-against-the-government-oftentimes-you-fall-hard/?sh=6ed1d29560cc. Accessed 10.05.2021.

Henig, D. (2021). *Global Trade Today Is Global Value Chains*. S.l.: ECIPE.

Henig, D., & Guildea, A. (2021). *Services Trade Needs to Be Taken as Seriously as Goods Trade*. New Globalization Project. European Centre for International Political Economy (ECIPE), Belgium 2021.

Herger, N., & McCorriston, S. (2013). On discrete location choice models. *Economics Letters*, 120(2), 288–291.

Hill, H., & Jongwanich, J. (2009). Outward foreign direct investment and the financial crisis in developing East Asia. *Asian Development Review*, 26(2), 1–25.

Hjálmarsdóttir, H. B., & Kristjánsdóttir, H. (2022, forthcoming). Marketing tourism. *Journal of Risk and Financial Management*.

Hüpponen, M. (2021). Interview with Mikko Hüpponen. *Talks with Petri*. www.youtube.com/watch?v=omfHKp0jlwE

ICEX. (2021). *Investment Trends and Records in Spain*. www.investinspain.org/en/publications. Accessed 22.09.2021.

IMF. (2020). China's GDP could overtake the United States by 2030. *Issues in Tourism*, 24(6), 738–741. doi:10.1080/13683500.2020.1734550

Ingham, T. (2020). Tencent, set to control 10% of Universal, also owns 9.1% of Spotify – but Daniel Ek has the final say on firm's stake, MusicBusinessWorldwide.com, published 10February2020,https://www.musicbusinessworldwide.com/tencent-set-to-control-10-of-universal-also-owns-9-1-of-spotify-but-daniel-ek-has-the-final-say-on-firms-stake/

Jain, Rajendra K. (2014). India-EU strategic partnership: Perceptions and perspectives. NFG Working Paper Series, No. 10, July 2014, NFG Research Group "Asian Perceptions of the EU" Freie Universität Berlin, pp. 1–25.

Jeakins, R. (2015). [Online] www.linkedin.com/pulse/supplier-jaguar-land-rover-subsidiary-strategy-central-robert-jeakins. Accessed 05.10.2021.

JETRO. (2020a). 2020 nendo Kaigai Shinshutsu Nikkei Kigyo no Jittai Chousa Oushu-hen (2020 Survey of Japanese Companies Operating Overseas in Europe).

JETRO. (2020b). Sekai Boueki Toushi Doukou Shirizu: Spain (World Trade and Investment Trends Series: Spain). www.jetro.go.jp/ext_images/world/gtir/2020/36.pdf. Assessed 20.09.2021.

Jia, K., & Kenney, M. (2021). The Chinese platform business group: An alternative to the Silicon Valley model. *Journal of Chinese Governance*, 1–23.

Jia, K., Kenney, M., & Zysman, J. (2018). Global competitors? Mapping the internationalization strategies of Chinese digital platform firms. In *International Business in the Information and Digital Age* (pp. 187–215). Bingley: Emerald Publishing Limited. https://doi.org/10.1108/S1745-886220180000013009

Jiang, Y., Zestos, G.K, Timmerman, Z. (2020). A Vector Error Correction Model for Japanese Real Exports, Atlantic Economic Journal, Springer;International Atlantic Economic Society, vol. 48(3), pages 297–311, September, DOI: 10.1007/s11293-020-09675-1.

Josh, Y. (2021a). China moves to protect food delivery drivers from digital exploitation, knocking stocks such as local services giant Meituan. *South China Morning Post.* www.scmp.com/tech/big-tech/article/3142588/china-moves-protect-food-delivery-drivers-digital-exploitation. Accessed 10.05.2021.

Josh, Y. (2021b). China limits gaming time for under-18s to one hour a day on Fridays, Saturdays, Sundays and public holidays. *South China Morning Post.* www.scmp.com/tech/policy/article/3146918/china-limits-gaming-time-under-18s-one-hour-day-fridays-saturdays. Accessed 10.05.2021.

Kajander, P. (2021). Semi-structured interview with Petri Kajander, start-up entrepreneur and business artist. September 27. Conducted virtually via Teams.

Katz, M. L., & Shapiro, C. (1994). Systems competition and network effects. *Journal of Economic Perspectives*, 8(2), 93–115.

Kaushal, L. A. (2018). Outward foreign direct investment: The Indian experience. *Transnational Corporations Review*, 10(1), 86–97. doi: 10.1080/19186444.2018.1436658. Accessed 13.05.2020.

Kawashima, S. (2020). Is Japan pulling its companies out of China?, A recent Japanese government policy is significant, but hardly a decoupling. *Tokyo Report*, May 11. https://thediplomat.com/2020/05/is-japan-pulling-its-companies-out-of-china/. Accessed 19.06.2020.

Keane, J. (2021). Wolt attracts scrutiny of its courier employment status in Finland. *Forbes*, August 3. www.forbes.com/sites/jonathankeane/2021/08/03/wolt-attracts-scrutiny-of-its-courier-employment-status-in-finland/?sh=140525c577ad

Keith, D. (2016). Stop TTIP: Towards a transnational Eurosceptic opposing the transatlantic trade and investment partnership? In *Euroscepticism as a Transnational and Pan-European Phenomenon* (pp. 111–126). Abingdon, UK: Routledge.

Kenney, M., & Pon, B. (2011). Structuring the smartphone industry: Is the mobile internet OS platform the key? *Journal of Industry, Competition and Trade*, 11(3), 239–261.

Kenney, M., & Zysman, J. (2016). The rise of the platform economy. *Issues in Science and Technology*, 32(3), 61.

Kenney, M., & Zysman, J. (2020). The platform economy: Restructuring the space of capitalist accumulation. *Cambridge Journal of Regions, Economy and Society*, 13(1), 55–76.

Kenney, M., Zysman, J., & Bearson, D. (2020). Transformation or structural change? What polanyi can teach us about the platform economy. *Sociologica*, 14(3), 227–240.

Ketenci, N. (2016). *The bilateral trade flows of the EU in the presence of structural breaks*. Empirical Economics, 51, 1369–1398.

Khanna, T., & Rivkin, J. W. (2001). Estimating the performance effects of business groups in emerging markets. *Strategic Management Journal*, 22, 45–74. http://dx.doi.org/10.1002/1097-0266(200101)

Kitsing, M. (2021). *The Political Economy of Digital Ecosystems: Scenario Planning for Alternative Futures*. New York: Routledge.

Klodt, H. (1993). Technology-based trade and multinationals' investment in Europe: Structural change and competition in Schumpeterian goods. In M. W. Klein & P. J. J. Welfens (Eds.), *Multinationals in the New Europe and Global Trade*. Berlin: Springer.

Kratz, A., Huotari, M., Hanemann, T., & Arcesati, R. (2020). Chinese FDI in Europe: 2019 update. *MERICS*, April 8, 2020. https://merics.org/en/report/chinese-fdi-europe-2019-update. Accessed 29.06.2020.

Kristjánsdóttir, H. (2021). Tax on tourism in Europe: Does higher value-added tax (VAT) impact tourism demand in Europe? *Current Issues in Tourism*, 24(6), 738–741, doi: 10.1080/13683500.2020.1734550

Kristjánsdóttir, H. (2013). Foreign direct investment in a small open economy. *Applied Economics Letters*, 20(15), 1423–1425. doi: 10.1080/13504851.2013.815306

Kristjánsdóttir, H. (2017). Country competitiveness: An empirical study. *Baltic Region*, 9(2), 31–44. doi: 10.5922/2079-8555-2017-2-3

Kristjánsdóttir, H. (2019a). Does investment replace aid as countries become more developed? *Baltic Journal of Economic Studies*, 5(2), 256–261. doi: 10.30525/2256-0742/2019-5-2-256-261

Kristjánsdóttir, H. (2019b). Tourism in a remote Nordic region: VAT, internet, oil, English, distance, Hofstede, and Christianity. *Cogent Social Sciences*, 5, 1709346. https://doi.org/10.1080/23311886.2019.1709346

Kristjánsdóttir, H., Guðjónsson, S., & Óskarsson, G. K. (2022). Free Trade Agreement (FTA) with China and interaction between exports and imports. *Baltic Journal of Economic Studies*, 8(1).

Kristjánsdóttir, H., Guðlaugsson, T., Guðmundsdóttir, S., & Aðalsteinsson, G. D. (2017). Hofstede national culture and international trade. *Applied Economics*, 49(57), 5792–5801. doi: 10.1080/00036846.2017.1343446

Kristjánsdóttir, H., Guðlaugsson, T., Guðmundsdóttir, S., & Aðalsteinsson, G. D. (2020). Cultural and geographical distance: Effects on UK exports. *Applied Economics Letters*, 27(4), 275–279. doi: 10.1080/13504851.2019.1613495

Kristjánsdóttir, H., & Karlsdóttir, F. B. (2020). UK foreign direct investment in the OECD, culture and geography. *Baltic Journal of Economic Studies*, 6(5), 8–14. https://doi.org/10.30525/256-0742/2020-6-5-8-14

Kristjánsdóttir, H., & Kristjánsdóttir, S. (2021). CarbFix and SulFix in geothermal production, and the Blue Lagoon in Iceland. *Baltic Journal of Economic Studies*, 7(1), 1–9. https://doi.org/10.30525/2256-0742/2021-7-1-1-9

Kristjánsdóttir, H., & Óskarsdóttir, S. (2021). European FDI in Ireland and Iceland: Before and after the financial crisis. *Journal of Risk and Financial Management*, 14(1), 23.

Kruskal, W. H., & Wallis, W. A. (1952). Use of ranks in one-criterion variance analysis. *Journal of the American Statistical Association*, 47(260), 583–621.

Kutlina-Dimitrova, Z. (2021). The impact of COVID-19 on exports related jobs. *Trade: Chief Economist Note*, 1(1), 1–17.

Lambiotte, R., Delvenne, J.-C., & Barahona, M. (2014). Random walks, Markov processes and the multiscale modular organization of complex networks. *IEEE Transactions on Network Science and Engineering*, 1(2), 76–90. https://doi.org/10.1109/TNSE.2015.2391998

Lanteigne, M. (2010). Northern exposure: Cross-regionalism and the China-Iceland preferential trade negotiations. *The China Quarterly*, 202, 362–380.

La Porta, R., Lopez-de-Silanes, F., Shleifer, A., & Vishny, R. (1997). Legal determinants of external finance. *Journal of Finance*, 52(3), 1131–1150.

Lindman, M. (2021). Semi-structured interview with Martin Lindman, CEO of Doktor.se. September 27. Conducted virtually via Teams.

Lipsey, R. E. (2002). Home and host country effects of FDI. Working Paper 9293, pp. 1–78. http://www.nber.org/papers/w9293

Lucas, R. (1988). On the mechanics of economic development. *Journal of Monetary Economics*, 22(1), 3–42, North Holland.

Ma, W., Abkowitz, A., & Steinberg, J. (2017). *Tencent Music, Spotify in Talks to Swap Stakes Ahead of Planned Listings*. www.wsj.com/articles/tencent-music-spotify-in-talks-to-swap-stakes-ahead-of-planned-public-listings-1512122042

Magnusson. (2021). *The Impact of New FDI Screening Rules in the Nordics and Baltics*. Online seminar on August 24.

Markusen, J., & Venables, A. (1998). Multinational firms and the new trade theory. *Journal of International Economics*, 46(2), 183–203.

Mátyás, L. (1998). The gravity model: Some econometric considerations. *World Economy*, 21(3), 397–401.

Mayes, Joe. (2021). U.K. starts prep for India trade deal in latest post-brexit push. *Bloomberg*, May 24, 23:30 CEST. www.bloomberg.com/news/articles/2021-05-24/u-k-starts-prep-for-india-trade-deal-in-latest-post-brexit-push. Accessed 12.07.2021.

McKenzie, M. D. (1999). The impact of exchange rate volatility on international trade flows. *Journal of Economic Surveys*, 13, 71–104.

McKnight, S., Kenney, M., & Breznitz, D. (2021). Platformizing the economy? Building and regulating Chinese digital platforms. SSRN Working Paper, July 12.

Ministerio de Industria, Comercio y Turismo. (2021). *Flujos de Inversiones Exteriores Directas 2020*. https://comercio.gob.es/InversionesExteriores/Publicaciones/Histrico%20de%20boletines/Ultimas%20publicaciones/Flujos-Inversion-Directa-Ultima-Publicacion.pdf. Accessed 22.09.2021.

Ministry of Foreign Affairs. (2020). *Annual Report of Statistics on Japanese Nationals Overseas*. www.mofa.go.jp/mofaj/toko/page22_003338.html. Accessed 9.09.2021.

Morris, S., & Palakh, J. (2016). *Determinants of Outward FDI: Empirical Analysis of OECD Source Countries*. https://ssrn.com/abstract=2733040 or http://dx.doi.org/10.2139/ssrn.2733040. Accessed 13.05.2020.

Moslares, C., & Ekanayake, E. M. (2018). The effect of real exchange rate volatility on exports in the Baltic region. *The International Journal of Business and Finance Research*, 12(1), 23–38.

Mukhopadhyay, K., & Thomassin, P. J. (2010). *Economic and Environmental Impact of Free Trade in East and South East Asia* (pp. 23–40). The Netherlands: Springer.

Nael, V. (2021). *Njordlaw*. www.njordlaw.com/admission-estonian-japan-trading-company-shares-trading-nasdaq-baltic-alternative-market-first. Accessed 10.09.2021.

Nambisan, S., Zahra, S. A., & Luo, Y. (2019). Global platforms and ecosystems: Implications for international business theories. *Journal of International Business Studies*, 50(9), 1464–1486.

Narita, M. (2000). Foreign direct investment in Spain after 1992: Emergence of new rivals. *Economic Journal of Hokkaido University*, 29, 97–120.

Narita, M. (2016). Chokusetsu Toushi to Supein Keizai no Hensen (The evolution of foreign direct investment and Spanish economy). In T. Ushijima (Ed.), *Gendai Supein no Shosou (Various Aspects of Modern Spain)*. Tokyo: Akashi Shoten.

Narita, M. (2021). Japanese FDI in Spain: Why do Japanese firms locate in Catalonia? In P. K. Biswas & R. Dygas (Eds.), *Asian Foreign Direct Investment in Europe*, Chap. 6. Abingdon: Routledge.

Natsiopoulos, K., & Tzeremes, N. (2021). *ARDL: ARDL, ECM and Bounds-Test for Cointegration*. Package version 0.1.1. https://CRAN.R-project.org/package=ARDL

Neves, A., Becker, W., & Dominguez-Toreiro, M. (2019). Explained, the economic ties between Europe and Asia. *World Economic Forum*. www.weforum.org/agenda/2019/05/ways-asia-and-europe-together-connected/. Accessed 18.05.2020.

Niko. (2021). *Tencent's Silent Pursuit of Global Gaming Domination*, May. https://nikopartners.com/tencents-silent-pursuit-of-global-gaming-domination/

Noe, T. H., & Parker, G. G. (2005). Winner take all: Competition, strategy and structure in the internet economy. *Journal of Economics and Management Strategy*, 14(1), 141–164.

North, D. (1990). *Institutions, Institutional Change and Economic Performance* (Political Economy of Institutions and Decisions). Cambridge: Cambridge University Press.

OECD. (2020). *OECD Foreign Direct Investment Regulatory Restrictiveness Index*. Paris, France: OECD.

Oriola. (2021). *Oriola Sells Part of Its Ownership in an e-Health Provider Doctor.se in Sweden*, May 31. www.oriola.com/news-and-releases/stock-exchange-releases/2021/oriola-sells-part-of-its-ownership-in-an-e-health-provider-doktor.se-in-sweden

Óskarsson, G. K., & Kristjánsdóttir, H. (2021). EU country and EFTA country export differences. *Journal of Risk and Financial Management*, 14(4), 147. https://doi.org/10.3390/jrfm14040147

Paprzycki, R., & Fukao, K. (2008). *Foreign Direct Investment in Japan: Multinationals' Role in Growth and Globalization*. Cambridge: Cambridge University Press.

Parker, G. G., & Van Alstyne, M. W. (2005). Two-sided network effects: A theory of information product design. *Management Science*, 51(10), 1494–1504.

Penrose, E. T. (1959). *A Theory of the Growth of the Firm*. New York: Wiley.

Perez, M. (2019). Tencent buys majority stake in "Clash of Clans" developer Supercell. *Forbes*, October 23. www.forbes.com/sites/mattperez/2019/10/23/tencent-buys-majority-stake-in-clash-of-clans-developer-supercell/?sh=4d02140f1c39

Pesaran, M. H., Shin, Y., & Smith, R. J. (2001). Bounds testing approaches to the analysis of level relationships. *Journal of Applied Econometrics*, 16, 289–326.

Phillips, P. C. B., & Perron, P. (1988). Testing for a unit root in time series regression. *Biometrika*, 75(2), 335–346.

PISM, The Polish Institute of International Affairs, Kugiel, P. (ed.), Berg, T., Biedermann, Z., Fürst, R., Horký-Hlucháň, O., Hornát, J., Kałan, D., Majer, M., Němec, J., Ricz, J., Sárvári, B., Szczudlik, J., Szunomár, Á., Wąsiński, M., & Wnukowski, D. (2016). *V4 Goes Global: Exploring Opportunities and Obstacles in the Visegrad's Countries Cooperation with Brazil, India, China and South Africa*. www.pism.pl/files/?id_plik=21522. Accessed 06.07.2021.

Plummer, M. G. (2002). EU and ASEAN: Real integration and lessons in financial cooperation. *World Economy*, 25(10), 1469–1500.

Pöyhönen, P. (1963). A tentative model for the volume of trade between countries. *Weltwirtschaftliches Archiv*, 90, 93–99.

Pradhan, J. P., & Neelam, S. (2008). Outward FDI and knowledge flows: A study of the Indian automotive sector. *International Journal of Institutions and Economies*, 1(1), 155–186.

Prakash, R., & Subrahmanya, T. (2015). *FDI and a Borderless World of Trade and Industry: Challenges and Opportunities*, Amazon Kindle.

Przychodniak, M. (2020). China and the Visegrad group: Transformation and future of the cooperation. Ośrodek Myśli Politycznej, USA-UE strona o stosunkach międzynarodowych, Teksty i komentarze. https://usa-ue.pl/teksty-i-komentarze/english/china-and-the-visegrad-group-transformation-and-future-of-the-cooperation/. Accessed 13.07.2021.

Rajendra, K. J. (2014). India-EU strategic partnership: Perceptions and Perspectives? NFG Working Paper No. 10/2014, NFG Research Group "Asian Perceptions of the EU" Freie Universität Berlin, pp. 8–9. https://citeseerx.ist.psu.edu/viewdoc/download?doi=10.1.1.1034.1966&rep=rep1&type=pdf. Accessed 13.07.2021.

Ramachandran, J., Khorakiwala, H. F., Rao, J., Khera, P., Dawar, N., Kalyani, B. N., & Karki, R. (2004). Indian companies in overseas markets: Perspectives, patterns, and implications. *Vikalpa: The Journal for Decision Makers*, 29(4), 93–111.

Razin, A., & Sadka, E. (2012). *Foreign Direct Investment: Analysis of Aggregate Flows* (1st ed.). Princeton: Princeton University Press.

Regulation (EU). (2019/452). European Parliament and of the council of 19 of March 2019 establishing a framework for the screening of foreign direct investments into the Union. *Official Journal of the European Union L*, 79 I/1, 6–8.

Rochet, J. C., & Tirole, J. (2006). Two-sided markets: A progress report. *The RAND Journal of Economics*, 37(3), 645–667.

Rueda-Cantuche, J., Kerner, R., Cernat, L., & Ritola, V. (2016). Trade in services by GATS modes of supply: Statistical concepts and first EU estimates. *Chief Economist Paper*, 1–27.

Ruehl, M., & Riordan, P. (2021). Tencent boosts global investments as Beijing cracks down on gaming. *Financial Times*, September. www.ft.com/content/422e3bd4-6c0c-493c-b888-883d331a89b9. Accessed 10.05.2021.

Saito, J. (2017). *Why Is Japan's Inward FDI So Low?* Tokyo: JCER.

SciencesPo. (2019). *Distance*. http://econ.sciences-po.fr/thierry-mayer/data

Seawright, J. (2016). The case for selecting cases that are deviant or extreme on the independent variable. *Sociological Methods and Research*, 45(3). https://doi.org/10.1177/0049124116643556

Shatz, H. (2000). *The Location of US Multinational Affiliates* (Doctoral dissertation). Harvard: Harvard University.

Shin, Y., Yu, B., & Greenwood-Nimmo, M. (2014). Modelling asymmetric cointegration and dynamic multipliers in a nonlinear ARDL framework. In R. Sickels & W. C. Horrace (Eds.), *Festschrift in Honor of Peter Schmidt: Econometric Methods and Applications* (pp. 281–314). New York, NY: Springer.

SIRU, Strategic Investment Research Unit. (2020). Measures taken by Government of India to aid Businesses during COVID-19 lockdown. *Business Immunity Platform Resources United against COVID-19*, April 23. www.investindia.gov.in/bip/resources/measures-taken-government-india-aid-businesses-during-covid-19-lockdown. Accessed 16.07.2021.

Stone, I. (1999). East Asian FDI and the UK periphery. In P. Garrahan & J. Ritchie (Eds.), *East Asian Direct Investment in UK* (pp. 59–95) (Studies in Asia Pacific Business no 6). London: Frank Cass Publishers.

Strittmatter, K. (2020). Chiny 5.0. *Jak powstaje cyfrowa dyktatura*, Grupa Wydawnicza Foksal Sp. z o. o, Wydanie 1. p. 16.

Subramanian, A., & Wei, S. J. (2007). The WTO promotes trade, strongly but unevenly. *Journal of International Economics*, 72(1), 151–175.

Talamo, G. (2007). Institutions, FDI, and the gravity model. Economic Growth, Institutional and Social Dynamics, Volume in Workshop PRIN 2005 SU, pp. 25–27.

Thomsen, S., Misuzu, O., & Boram, L. (2011). The evolving role of Southeast Asia in global FDI flows, Asie. Vision 40, Ifri Centre for Asian Studies, June.

Tinbergen, J. (1962). *Shaping the World Economy: Suggestions for an International Economic Policy*. New York, NY: The Twentieth Century Fund.

Tolentino, P. E. (2008), The determinants of the outward foreign direct investment of China and India: Whither the home country?, No 2008-049. MERIT Working Papers, United Nations University – Maastricht Economic and Social Research Institute on Innovation and Technology (MERIT).

Turrión, J. (2005). El Impacto de la Ampliación en los Flujos de Inversión Directa. *Papeles de Economía Española*, 103, 157–171.

UN Comtrade Database. (2021). *Data*. https://comtrade.un.org/data/

UNCTAD. (2001). *World Investment Report: Promoting Linkages, United Nations Conference on Trade and Development 2001*. Geneva and New York.

UNCTAD. (2019). *UNCTAD Handbook Statistics 2019: Economic Trends*. https://unctad.org/en/PublicationChapters/tdstat44_FS09_en.pdf. Accessed 06.05.2020.

UNCTAD. (2020). *Handbook of Statistics*. New York: United Nations Publications.

UNCTAD. (2020a). Impact of the COVID-19 pandemic on global FDI and GVCs updated analysis. *Global Investment Trend Monitor No 35*, March 23. https://unctad.org/en/pages/newsdetails.aspx?OriginalVersionID=2313. Accessed 06.05.2020.

UNCTAD. (2020b). *World Investment Report 2020, International Production beyond the Pandemic, Key Messages and Overview*. https://unctad.org/en/PublicationsLibrary/wir2020_overview_en.pdf. Accessed 01.07.2020.

UNCTAD. (2021a). *World Investment Report 2021: Investing in Sustainable Recovery*. New York: United Nations Publications.

UNCTAD. (2021b). *World Investment Report*. New York: UNCTAD.

United Nations (Ed.). (2012). *Manual on Statistics of International Trade in Services 2010: MSITS 2010* (Rev. ed). United Nations. ISBN 978-92-1-161542-5.

Upadhyaya, K. P., Dhakal, D., & Mixon, F. G. (2020). Exchange rate volatility and exports: Some new estimates from the ASEAN-5. *The Journal of Developing Areas*, 54, 65–73.

Van Dijck, J., Poell, T., & De Waal, M. (2018). *The Platform Society: Public Values in a Connective World*. Oxford: Oxford University Press.

Van Tulder, R., Carneiro, J., & Gonzalez-Perez, M. A. (2016). *Introduction* to *This Volume: What Makes BRIC Multinationals the Challenge of Bric Multinationals* (pp. 41–57). Bingley: Emerald Group Publishing Limited. https://doi.org/10.1108/S1745-886220160000011005

Vesterbacka, P. (2021). *Presentation at the New Campus Opening of EBS Helsinki*, August 16. Helsinki, Finland.

Wagner, T. (2018). *Data Stories: One Billion Euro Public EU Money Awarded to Chinese Companies*. https://yourdatastories.eu/datastories-one-billion-euro-public-eu-money-awarded-to-chinese-companies/. Accessed 29.06.2020.

Wang, Y., & Coe, N. M. (2021). Platform ecosystems and digital innovation in food retailing: Exploring the rise of Hema in China. *Geoforum*, 126, 310–321.

Welfens, P. (1997). Privatization, structural change and productivity: Towards convergence in Europe? In S. Black (Ed.), *Europe's Economy Looks East* (pp. 212–257). Cambridge: Cambridge University Press.

Welfens, P., Knipping, F., Chirathivat, S., & Ryan, C. (2006). Integration in Asia and Europe Historical dynamics, political issues, and economic perspectives. doi: 10.1007/3-540-28730-2

Wettstein, S., Liberatore, A., Magdeleine, J., & Maurer, A. (2019). *A Global Trade in Services Data Set by Sector and by Mode of Supply*. Geneva: World Trade Organization.

Williamson, O. E. (1975). *Markets and Hierarchies*. New York: Free Press.

Witkowska, J. (2013). Foreign direct investment between Asian developing countries and the EU member states: The role of integration processes, comparative economic research. *Central and Eastern Europe*, 16(2). doi: 10.2478/cer-2013-0009

World Bank (2021). Open Data. Obtained from https://data.worldbank.org Accessed 15.09.2021.

World Economic Forum. (2019). *Global Competitiveness Report 2019*. www.weforum.org. Accessed 15.09.2021.

WTO. (1995). *General Agreement on Trade in Services*. Geneva: WTO.

Wyles, R., Fraser, S., & Bell, D. (2013). *Efficiency and Transparency: Jaguar Land Rover*. [Online]. www.pwc.co.uk/assets/pdf/delivering-client_value-jaguar-land-rover.pdf. Accessed 05.10.2021.

Wyrzykowska, M. (2010). *Bezpośrednie inwestycje zagraniczne w "nowych krajach" Unii Europejskiej – na przykładzie Polski*, Toruńskie Studia Międzynarodowe. Międzynarodowe Stosunki Ekonomiczne nr 1(3).

Xinmei, S. (2021). China issues tighter data security rules for ride-hailing firms amid Didi probe, but more clarity still needed. *South China Morning Post*. www.scmp.com/tech/policy/article/3146051/china-issues-tighter-data-security-rules-ride-hailing-firms-amid-didi. Accessed 10.05.2021.

Yixiao, J., Zestos, G. K., & Timmerman, Z. (2020). A vector error correction model for Japanese real exports. *Atlantic Economic Journal*, 48, 297–311.

Zeileis, A., Leisch, F., Hornik, K., & Kleiber, C. (2002). Strucchange: An R package for testing for structural change in linear regression models. *Journal of Statistical Software*, 7(2), 1–38.

Zeileis, C., Kleiber, W., & Hornik, K. (2003). Testing and dating of structural changes in practice. *Computational Statistics & Data Analysis*, 44, 109–123.

Zhang, J., & Chen, C. (2021). Alibaba antitrust investigation: What is the "picking one from the two" practice that triggered an official probe? *South China Morning Post*. www.scmp.com/tech/enterprises/article/3115300/alibaba-antitrust-investigation-what-picking-one-two-practice. Accessed 10.05.2021.

Zhang, Y., Hu, Y., & Luo, M. (2021). Exclusive: Tencent ordered to set up financial holding company. *Caixin*. www.caixinglobal.com/2021-05-26/exclusive-tencent-ordered-to-set-up-financial-holding-company-101718352.html. Accessed 10.05.2021.

Data source

https://ec.europa.eu/eurostat, Eurostat database, accessed 10.09.2021

www.fdiintelligence.com, accessed 06.09.2021

https://andmed.stat.ee/en/stat/majandus__valiskaubandus__teenuste_valiskaubandus/VKT13/table/tableViewLayout1, accessed 05.10.2021

https://ec.europa.eu/digital-single-market/en/digital-economy-and-society-index-desi

https://ec.europa.eu/eurostat/statistics-explained/index.php?title=File:EU_trade_balance_of_goods_with_India,_2020.png#file, accessed 08.07.2021

www.hcltech.com/press-releases/it-infrastructure-management/gartner-recognizes-hcl-leader-managed-workplace-services, accessed 25.09.2021

https://static.www.tencent.com/uploads/2021/04/08/960eae1f18dd716fd3a7d704e123d7a5.pdf), accessed 07.10.2021

https://unctadstat.unctad.org/wds/TableViewer/tableView.aspx?ReportId=96740, accessed 05.10.2021

https://unctadstat.unctad.org/wds/TableViewer/tableView.aspx?ReportId=96740, accessed 05.10.2021

https://unctadstat.unctad.org/wds/TableViewer/tableView.aspx?ReportId=135718, accessed 05.10.2021

www.accord-healthcare.com/, accessed 25.09.2021

www.autocarpro.in/news-international/tata-jlr-journey-billion-pounds-billion-pounds-29749, 25.09.2021

www.businessinsider.in/business/auto/news/tata-motors-is-the-casualty-of-jlr-struggling-due-to-the-global-chip-shortage-and-a-lacklustre-ev-vision/articleshow/85652897.cms, accessed 25.09.2021

www.business-standard.com/article/news-cm/tata-motors-jlr-to-temporarily-suspend-production-at-2-uk-plants-121042300235_1.html, accessed 25.09.2021

www.cii.in/PublicationDetail.aspx?enc=1agwryCtEz7DIq63Mjvd77H6ddn/A0Y6Aqn3S6QSrv78SsoZthdV1q/9fJM1K2do7HDJd0s+Z8Xgj/fTd81ZG620q7Wx3+85gxh+SxCpVilNLEHy0DzSGsYVuJNWW7qxQN2+0LJiA7/4GpyQ6ufP0j8Mo89fYmQLapUGpGmJ+dnIbk4TNwWhQXSaJ9OLXMrQ, accessed 03.09.2021

www.cii.in/PublicationDetail.aspx?enc=egwqkqCFh440zDDIpfQpIafVjUXSQ6t6thWFGzPgipFJeaBtKyEWZn0i6RKYsjaSMOfezkCsOc/2nQ1up6tCCnCJv41jG70eg5vfMEoVajaEPtUtTj8WZuhVfSKIxXZ5T9ZeQY1MK42VlN/OumCw3N0j1HYFc0RWUAoEb7nJ6RhSLi0KhCJRno5tJUNGg5RU, accessed 03.09.2021

www.cii.in/PublicationDetail.aspx?enc=PDe4p+aFEDts+HMT20oM6lLTLF6fp28je3uUfHAs/0K99bVfSsOk8WfGuiioDv5PCdMG9bimJS3FdKopeIHrfV7XlyLCIrKoydZ4

KpKOZsLK4RiqCZcMEeUDAoQOB2Kh8JP5Ml1xJvlpi6/HmxOdhdd+SXHOqyNhq4dYuGo9VvXcB7CeLQi26QSSpjLd6v6z, accessed 03.09.2021
www.find-and-update.company-information.service.gov.uk/company/04596349/filing-history, accessed 26.09.2021
www.forbes.com/sites/neilwinton/2020/06/28/jaguar-future-at-risk-as-owner-tata-motors-ponders-jlr-recovery-plan/?sh=6d1afa5372fa, accessed 25.09.2021
www.gov.uk/government/collections/trade-and-investment-factsheets, accessed 23.09.2021
www.gov.uk/government/statistics/department-for-international-trade-inward-investment-results-2020-to-2021/department-for-international-trade-inward-investment-results-2020-to-2021-online-version, accessed 25.09.2021 www.ons.gov.uk/businessindustryandtrade/business/businessinnovation/datasets/foreigndirectinvestmentinvolvingukcompanies2013inwardtables, accessed 17.09.2021
www.gov.uk/government/statistics/trade-and-investment-factsheets-partner-names-beginning-with-g-to-i, accessed 21.09.2021
www.grantthornton.in/en/insights/articles/india-meets-britain-tracker-2018/, accessed 03.092021
www.grantthornton.in/en/insights/articles/india-meets-britain-tracker-2020/, accessed 03.09.2021
www.grantthornton.in/en/insights/articles/india-meets-britain-tracker-2021/, accessed 03.09.2021
www.grantthornton.in/en/insights/articles/indian-companies-contribution-to-the-uk-economy-surges/, accessed 03.09.2021
www.hcltech.com/geo-presence/united-kingdom, accessed 25.09.2021
www.hcltech.com/press-releases/awards-recognitions/hcl-top-employer-uk-twelfth-consecutive-year, accessed 25.09.2021
www.hcltech.com/press-releases/press-releases-business/hcl-expands-investment-united-kingdom, accessed 25.09.2021
www.investindia.gov.in/, accessed 25.09.2021
www.jaguarlandrover.com/, accessed 24.09.2021
www.jaguarlandrover.com/investor-relations, accessed 25.09.2021
www.jaguarlandrover.com/reimagine, accessed 25.09.2021
www.jetro.go.jp/ext_images/_Reports/01/7fc638152f5b8915/20200016.pdf, accessed 09.09.2021
www.mnacritique.mergersindia.com/what-convinced-tata-motors-to-take-over-the-jlr/, accessed 28.09.2021
www.ons.gov.uk/businessindustryandtrade/business/businessinnovation/datasets/foreigndirectinvestmentinvolvingukcompanies2013inwardtables, accessed 02.09.2021
www.securemeters.com/about-us/our-history/, accessed 16.09.2021
www.securemeters.com/in/about-us/innovation/#1590055724107-d7b0d277-07b1, accessed 16.09.2021
www.securemeters.com/uk/about-us/our-brands/, accessed 16.09.2021
www.securemeters.com/uk/about-us/what-we-do/operations/, 16.09.2021
www.securemeters.com/uk/beanbag_services/beanbag-care/, accessed 17.09.2021
www.tata.com/business/jlr, accessed 24.09.2021
www.uk.globaldatabase.com/company/accord-healthcare-limited, accessed 25.09.2021
www.uk.globaldatabase.com/company/secure-meters-uk-limited, accessed 28.09.2021
www.webarchive.nationalarchives.gov.uk/ukgwa/20160105184457/http:/www.ons.gov.uk/ons/rel/international-transactions/outward-foreign-affiliates-statistics/the-uk-s-trade-and-investment-relationship-with-india/sty-india.html, accessed 23.09.2021

www.imf.org/en/Publications/WEO/weo-database/2021/April, IMF, World Economic Outlook database, April 202, accessed 10.09.2021

www.jetro.go.jp/en/reports/statistics.html, JETRO, Trade and Investment Statistics accessed 10.09.2021

http://datainvex.comercio.es, Ministerio de Industria, Comercio y Turismo, DataInvex accessed 20.09.2021

www.customs.go.jp/toukei/info/index_e.htm, Ministry of Finance, Trade Statistics of Japan, accessed 15.09. 2021

www.oecd.org OECD (2019), accessed 21.06.2021

www.worldbank.org/, World Bank (2021), accessed 21.06.2021

www.wto.org/english/res_e/statis_e/its_e.htm, WTO (2015). International Trade Statistics 2000–2015 [PDF version], accessed 21.06.2021

www.grantthornton.in/en/insights/articles/india-meets-britain – tracking-the-uks-top-indian-companies/, accessed 03.09.2021

Index